SAP XI Transaction Codes:

SAP Exchange Infrastructure Certification Review

By Gajendra Bhakuni

SAP XI Transaction Codes: SAP Exchange Infrastructure
Certification Review

ISBN 13: 9781-933804-99-6

Please visit our website at www.sapcookbook.com

TABLE OF CONTENTS

Introduction:

Almost everyday, new IT landscapes of varying degrees are introduced to the global market. Due to a wide array of software used to create IT landscapes, the issue of integration among the varied systems has become a problem. Connectivity, formatting differences, and protocol disparities are just some of the requirements that need to be addressed. Most individuals and businesses will want to retain their old IT system in the face of new developments in the field. A preference for a well-known system is easily explained; due to the huge volume of data the system has accumulated a translation to a new system often means a lot of work. It is often not cost effective to simply replace an existing system with the one that the market demands. Often times, it will take thousands of dollars, if not millions (for very big companies) to make the shift to a new IT landscape, and that cost just covers the initial change of system. The thousands of dollars invested in a new system still do not include the cost to train the required personnel to handle the new system or the time involved in the learning process.

An answer to the problem faced by many companies is the SAP Exchange Infrastructure (SAP XI) component. SAP XI is a powerful integration broker that smoothly integrates connectivity, format and protocol requirements of various IT landscapes, even adapting to software made by other companies. It supports cross-component business process management (BPM) within the same solution. In addition, it is a component of the SAP Netweaver platform and runs on the SAP Web Application Server.

SAP XI provides a common, central repository for different interfaces, thereby reducing the costs of integration and maintenance of multiple IT systems. SAP XI offers an integrated tool set that helps individuals or organizations build their own scenarios by defining messaging interfaces, mappings, and routing rules. It also supports multiple communication approaches like peer-to-peer connections and central hubs. SAP XI reduces the cost of integration by letting an individual or organization use existing components, for example pre-existing investments in electronic data interchange (EDI). SAP XI seamlessly integrates components from both SAP and third-party vendors for smooth information interchange.

SAP XI offers a wide variety of different prepackaged integration content in order to address the different needs of individual consumers. In SAP XI specific business content is addressed, for example data types, message types, interface description, business scenarios, and process patterns are included. SAP XI also offers complete solutions for business problems without compromising the quality that matches industry standards. The SAP XI integration repository is open to third party and custom content, allowing the component to serve as the centralized location for all integration content. SAP XI also allows you to model cross component business processes and scenarios, which allows the consumer to control complex business processes across business applications. This covers the full process life cycle, including design, automation, execution, and monitoring. It is even possible to automate processes that will suite every unique need of your business or corporation.

TABLES IN XI

Pipeline related:

a) SXMSPADM - XMS Pipeline: Execution Settings. Indicates whether the pipeline is enabled/disabled.
b) SXMSPCONF - Administrative Data for Pipeline Configuration.
c) SXMSPIPE - XML Message Server: Pipeline Definition. Pipeline and the type of pipeline (Process Engine, Runtime and Acknowledgement) are indicated.
d) SXMSPIPEEL - For each pipeline ID the pipeline steps and Pipeline service Identifier can be found.
e) SXMSPLSRV – Further details regarding Pipeline Service can be found here. Pipeline service is the service called during processing of an XML message within the pipeline of an Integration engine.

Tip: Pipeline definition can also be reached via transaction SXMB_ADM -> Display Pipeline Definition.

Archiving related:

The following large tables need to be archived regularly:

Those that contain the XI message related data:
a) SXMSCLUP - XMB: Property Cluster.
b) SXMSCLUR - XMB: Resources Cluster.
Note: For the above two cluster tables we can run the report RSXMB_DEL_CLUST_TABLE to delete entries.
c) SXMSPHIST - XML Message Broker: History.
d) SXMSPMAST - Integration Engine: Message Queue (Master).
Note: From table SXMSPMAST we can extract the message ID and from class CL_XMS_PERSIST, using its method read_msg_all we can extract the payload of the message.
e) SXMSPERROR – Message queue incorrect entries.

<u>Additional tables to be archived:</u>

f) SXMSPFRAWH - Integration Engine: Header Table for Raw Data for Performance Evaluation. This table includes GUIDs of senders and receivers.

g) SXMSPFADDRESS - Integration Engine: Sender and Receiver Information.

h) SXMSPFAGG - Integration Engine: Aggregated Data for Performance Display.

i) SXMSPFRAWD - Integration Engine: Data Table for Raw Data for Performance.

j) SWWWIHEAD - Workflow Runtime: Header Table for All Work Item Types. This table stores BPM related data.

k) SXMSPEMAS – Integration Engine: Enhanced Message Queue (Master).

l) SXMSPVERS - Integration Engine: Message Version.

m) SWFRXICNT - XI Adapter: XML Container for a Message Object.

n) SWFRXIHDR - XI Adapter: Header Data for a Message Object.

o) SWFRXIPRC - XI-Adapter: Process-Dependent Message Data.

<u>Cache Related:</u> *The following tables are referred by cache at runtime and contain data from Integration Directory – receiver determination, interface, mapping, routing, communication channel etc.*

a) TRD_RELATION - Meta Data for Receiver Determination.

b) TRD_RULE - Meta Data for condition based routing.

c) TRD_NAMESPACE - Meta Data for XPATH rules.

d) TRD_EXTRACTOR - Meta Data for containers used in ccBPM. XI Extractors.

e) SMPPREL3 - Meta Data for mapping runtime.

f) SMPPMAP3 - Meta Data for mapping runtime.

g) SMPPSPLIT - Meta Data for mapping runtime. Merge and split.

h) SXI_SWCV_LAYER - Meta Data for software component version.

i) SSRVBINDING - Meta Data for Service Bindings.

j) SSRVPARTY - Meta Data for Parties.

k) SSRVSERVICE - Meta Data for Services, Party Identifiers for a Service.

l) SSRVCHANNEL - Meta Data for Communication Channels.
m) SWFXICACHE - Meta Data for ccBPM's.
n) SWFXICLOG - Meta Data for ccBPM message logs.
o) SWFXIOBJS - Cache: Objects of a Process Definition (Proxy, CRL).
p) LCRT_CLNTCACHE – SLD data of the business system is cached in this table. This table is populated with the data from the first request for information.
Note: For manual invalidation of LCR cache use function module: LCR_CLEAR_CACHE.

XI Alerts:

a) SXMSALERTCONTROL – Control table for XI alerts.
b) SXMSALERTLOG – XI Alert log.
c) SXMSALERTLOG – XI Alert log.
d) SXMSALERTRULES - Rules for Alert Generation: Message Header -> Alert Category.
e) SXMSALERTTMSTMP - Time Stamp of Last PMI Process Instance Checked.

Miscellaneous:

a) SXMSCONFVL – Integration Engine configuration data.
b) SXMSCONFDF - Integration Engine Configuration parameters.
c) SXMSDCONF – Integration Engine: Settings for Deletion Concept
d) SXIPMIDEST – PMI Component and Destination for XI Component.
e) SXISLDAEC - XI: Cache for Adapter Engine Data from the SLD
f) SXMS_AE_AUDITCNF - XI: Adapter Runtime Data.
g) SXMSQUEUE RCV - Mapping Queue Receiver (XI service in ID).
h) SXMSSYERR – System error codes. Error categories and IDs.
i) LCRT_SERVADDR – Landscape directory server address.

j) IDXSNDPOR/IDXRCVPOR – Link between the IDoc adapter GUID and the IDoc number.
k) IDXEDSAPPL – IDoc adapter fields in the segments for each port.
l) IDXQUEUE – IDoc adapter queue.
m) IDXNOALE – For IDoc-XI-IDoc scenarios if you want to suppress any kind of acknowledgement then this table is maintained. This table specifies the port, the client of sender and the message type. Once this exception table has been maintained an acknowledgement will no longer be requested.

TRANSACTIONS IN XI

1) SXMB_IFR – Start Integration Builder.
   Tip: Builder does not immediately open up when running the transaction (http://hostname:port/rep/start/index.jsp) but must be opened as URL separately specifying the ip address (http://ipaddress:port/rep/start/index.jsp). Enter the ip address and hostname in the host file located at - **windows folder/system32/drivers/etc.** *Also ensure that the entry of XI is bypassed in the proxy server in Internet Explorer -> Tools -> Internet Options -> Connection -> Lan Settings -> Advanced.*

2) SXMB_MONI – Integration Engine monitoring.
   Tip: Cannot see the XI messages in the XI monitor for synchronous scenario. In the default setting of the integration engine synchronous messages are turned off, hence they are not displayed. To alter this it is necessary to switch logging and trace on in SXMB_ADM -> Integration Engine Configuration -> specific configuration -> Category RUNTIME for parameters: LOGGING, LOGGING_SYNC and TRACE_LEVEL.

3) SXMB_MONI_BPE – When an integration process is executed, the system creates the corresponding work items, as created during execution of SAP workflow. It is very difficult to monitor individual work items, as the relationship between work items is not quickly apparent. Hence this transaction provides a process oriented approach to monitor integration processes within XI. It contains the following:
   - Graphical overview of the process
   - Detailed list with process-related work items
   - Correlation identifier (if applicable)
   - Mapping (if applicable)

4) SXMB_ADM – Integration Engine: administration.

It offers the following:

<u>Configuration:</u>
1. Configure event-driven message processing – Using this engine, it is possible to control the processing of a message or message packages by means of a particular event.

2. Prioritized message processing – This differentiates messages with QOS (Quality of Service) – EO (Exactly once) or EOIO (Exactly Once in Order) according to their application case and prioritizes them.

3. Defining sender/receiver IDs that can be used in event driven message processing.

4. Configure Integration Engine:

   <u>Global configuration data</u> – This is primarily used to specify the role of the current business system (Integration server or application system).

   There can be only one Integration Server in an SAP system i.e. only one client

   (Business System) can be defined as: Integration Server.

5. <u>Local configuration data</u> – Functioning to further fine tune the business system, this defines various parameters and their values.

6. Displaying pipeline definition – Displays the pipeline steps that are performed during processing of XML message. Individual steps are called pipeline elements which in turn call exactly one pipeline service.

Note: Sometimes, runtime workbench message monitoring error messages appear multiple times even though the interface got triggered multiple times and there is only one message in SXMB_MONI. This often occurs when the IS_RETRY parameter is defined in administration.

Administration:
1.   Manage Queues – Register, Deregister and Activate Inbound/Outbound/Acknowledgement Queues.
2.   Archiving in XI

5)   SXMB_ADM_BPE – Process Engine administration.
SXMB_ADMIN – Integration Engine: All functions.
SXMS_SAMON – Monitor for synchronous/asynchronous communication to display status information about persisted messages where coupling of synchronous and asynchronous processing has occurred. It provides the following information:
The number of active synchronous calls still waiting for a response
The number of canceled processes (synchronous calls) whose status has not yet been deleted
A table containing status information about the involved synchronous request messages.

SXI_CACHE – XI Directory Cache. For performance reasons, and to keep the runtime components independent from the Integration Repository and Integration Directory, the ABAP runtime caches the following information:
Integration Directory and Repository data
Adapter engine connection data cache and CPA cache
IDoc adapter cache

SLD data.

To view the cached addresses of all Adapter Engines that are registered at the Integration Server, choose
Goto -> AE Cache

Tip: If software components versions are added or changed in SLD, the altered components will not be able to be selected in the Integration Repository unless the cache is forced to manually refresh.

6) SXI_MONITOR – Message monitoring in XI.

SXI_MAPPING_TEST – This function is used to test and debug maps based on the configuration details of a given scenario. Upon execution, it prompts to enter the message in XML format, which can be copied from SXI_MONITOR (for the erroneous message).

7) SXI_SHOW_MESSAGE – Displays an XI message.
8) SXI_DEMO – XI demo example: Travel Agency.
9) SXIPATT1 – This tests configurations by sending an XML message via XI after the configurations are done.
10) SMGW – Gateway monitor. This makes it possible to monitor the RFCs registered with the gateway (especially the sender RFCs which show a failure at the gateway). While configuring the sender RFC adapter the program ID needs to be registered at the gateway. Via this transaction it is possible to check which program IDs that are registered at the SAP gateway.

SPROXY –This is used to generate proxies out of the message interface (inbound/outbound) defined in Integration repository. The proxy generation converts non-language specific interface descriptions in WSDL into executable interfaces called proxies, which is the term used for executable interfaces in the application system.

Java proxies – When generated in IR from WSDL, these contain descriptions of interfaces. The results in are found in .jar files containing generated java classes.

ABAP proxies – These are generated in the application server with SPROXY transactions based on WSDL representation of message interface.
Note: For WAS release lower than 6.20 adapters are the only means to establish connections. From WAS 6.20 onward, a proxy generation feature enables application systems to communicate with XI using proxies. Proxies enable adapter-less communication (native connectivity).

<u>Some facts about proxies:</u>

<table>
<tr><td>

a) ABAP proxies are created in transaction SPROXY. This is executed on the Application system (not the Integration Server).

</td></tr>
<tr><td>

b) As part of configuration of WAS (Web Application Server), an HTTP destination to Integration Server is maintained in SM59.

</td></tr>
<tr><td>

c) Outbound message interface – client proxies
   Inbound message interface – server proxies.

</td></tr>
<tr><td>

d) The way to find the Web Application Server Client for the XI System is:

SXMB_IFR -> Administration -> All properties

</td></tr>
<tr><td>

e) As the code is client independent a proxy can be generated / writen anywhere. However, when executing the same it is not possible to do so from the same client as of the integration server.
To overcome this, make the following code change within class

```
CL_XMS_RUN_TIME_ENV -> CONSTRUCTOR


    METHOD constructor.
        IF parser IS INITIAL.
           CREATE OBJECT parser
           exporting im_property = me.
        ENDIF.


        proxy_allowed_on_is = ' '. "do not allow
    proxy on IS
              * proxy_allowed_on_is = 'X'. "allow
proxy on IS


        ENDMETHOD.
```

</td></tr>
</table>

11) RZ10 – Maintain profile parameters. This is used for performance tuning.

12) RZ20 – CCMS monitoring. Using this, a CCMS monitoring set can be created for the systems within the system group defined in RZ21.

<u>Workflow Related:</u>
13) SWF_XI_SWPR - Restart Workflow after error.
14) SWF_XI_CUSTOMIZING – Automatic customization of Business Process Engine. This process normally takes place during installation. It is important to note that all entries should be green in this transaction prior to configuring BPM. SWELS – Switch on/off event trace.
15) SWEL – Display event trace.
16) SWEQADM – Event Queue Administration. Check events. *Note: Most of the XI workflows are triggered by events (user WF-BATCH logs in).*
If the process does not start or message is not delivered to the started process then the cause might be that the event queue background job might not be running. Messages are delivered to process instances via events. In cases where events cannot be delivered the event is put into event queue (if active).
In order to resolve the problem, check this transaction to see if the background job is running.

<u>IDOC Related:</u>
17) IDX1 – Port maintenance in IDoc adapter.
In order to render IDoc-XML from IDoc, or the IDoc from IDoc-XML, the IDoc adapter must have access to the metadata underneath the IDoc definition. Since the IDoc metadata is stored in the application system, the Integration Server must retrieve this data via RFC callback. Transaction IDX1 is used to configure the port used for retrieving this data.
18) IDX2 - Meta data overview in IDoc adapter.
For scenarios where a business system sends to or receives from an IDoc from XI the settings in the above two transactions need to be done.
   - Transaction SM59 creates an RFC destination for the IDoc sender/receiver. This is used to retrieve the IDoc metadata from the sender/receiver system.
   - Using transaction IDX1 the port is assigned (RFC destination) to the system (client of the sender/receiver) that contains the metadata of the IDoc types.
   - Using transaction IDX2 the metadata for the IDoc type is loaded using the port defined in IDx1. If IDoc metadata changes in the source system then via IDX2

the old metadata can be deleted in preparation to reload the new one.

Note: The IDoc adapter only uses the service definition (business system) together with the corresponding adapter-specific identifiers in the Integration Directory. The maintenance of the IDoc sender system in the SLD is therefore not sufficient. It is recommended to assign a business system definition retrieved from the SLD to a service in the Integration Directory. Using this information about the system ID, client, and logical system name for a specific business system, the IDoc adapter is able to specify the corresponding service in the XML header. Routing is then based on service names.

Tip: How to correct error unable to convert sender service to an ALE logical system?

19) IDX5 – IDoc adapter monitoring. For IDoc scenarios it is possible to check whether the IDoc adapter received the IDoc or not. It can also be used to drill down and see if there is a problem related to tRFCs failure (like no proper authorization).
Check SAP note **940313** - IDoc adapter: Error messages in SM58 for details.
20) IDXPW – Activate IDoc message packages. This is where a used can specify the packet size by which the IDocs are cached in the IDoc adapter until the packet size is reached. On reaching the packet size the adapter triggers the entries.
21) IDXP – Monitor message packages. This location is used to monitor the IDoc message packages.
22) SCC4 – Client administration. Clients are assigned to a system as part of ALE partner profile configuration. The logical system name for the business system that is define in SLD must be same like in the corresponding SAP system.
23) WE20 – Maintain partner profile.
24) WE02/WE05 – Monitor IDocs.
25) WE19 – IDoc test tool.
26) SM59 – Maintain RFC destinations.
27) SALE – ALE settings.
28) BD64 – Maintain Distribution model.
29) WEINBQUEUE – Monitor transaction for IDoc inbound queue.
30) WEOUTQUEUE – Monitor transaction for IDoc outbound queue.

<u>Message Queue:</u>
Before starting with queue related transaction it is important to gain insight into.

31) SMQ1 – qRFC monitor (Outbound queue). Here, the status of inbound message queue can be monitored.
32) SMQ2 – qRFC monitor (Inbound queue). Here, the status of the outbound message queue can be monitored.
With the above two transactions the volume of qRFC queues (inbound or outbound) can be traced. For tRFC queues the volume cane be traced using transaction SM58.

Note: The message queue of the adapter framework is different from the queue of the Integration Server. The queue entries of the adapter framework cannot be seen in SMQ1/SMQ2. In order to monitor those, it is necessary to go to the message monitoring in runtime workbench.

33) SMQR – Registration of inbound tRFC/qRFC queues (Inbound Scheduler). This processes the inbound queues that are scheduled by QIN scheduler. The QIN Scheduler is available in all applications, and has been developed so that each application does not have to create its own Scheduler for automatic processing of the inbound queue.
34) SMQS – Registration of outbound tRFC/qRFC queues (Outbound Scheduler). The QOUT scheduler was implemented to improve the performance when sending qRFC and tRFC messages. A destination is registered automatically in the QOUT Scheduler if it is one of the following:
   - A destination for an external program (type T in SM59).
   - A destination for another SAP system (type 3 in SM59) and logon data (client, user, password, language) has been defined completely in transaction SM59).
Queues can be activated and deactivated in scheduler.

Tip: How to reprocess failed XI messages

35) SMQ3 – qRFC monitor (Save E-queue). If the queue processing gets stopped due to some erroneous message then save the problem entry queue message (LUW) in order that it

can be restarted at a later point in time via qRFC monitor.
- Go to the qRFC monitor to the queue ID
- Mark the LUW entry within the queue and use Edit – Save LUW.
- To restart it later, call transaction SMQ3, mark the entry and use Edit – Restore LUW.

36) SMQA – tRFC/qRFC: Confirm status and data. SM58 can be used for tRFC specifically.
37) SMQE – qRFC administration.
38) SXMSFILTER – Message filter maintenance.
39) SMICM – ICM monitor.
40) SICF – Monitoring and controlling communications. It includes the following functions for monitoring, analysis and troubleshooting:

- Activating Debugging

- Run traces

- Parsing URL

- ICF Recorder

Tip: Monitoring has negative effects on performance and should only be activated when necessary.
Note: Report RSXMB_ACTIVATE_ICF_SERVICES to activate ICF services.

Tip: Whenever a HTTP request is sent to XI using plain HTTP adapter a user is required to enter username and password each time for authentication. The username, password and language can be set globally in parameter sap/xi/adapter_plain to avoid giving credentials repeatedly.

SLD related:
41) SLDCHECK – Test SLD connection.
Access to exchange profile –
<<http://<xiserver>:<port>/exchangeProfile/index.html>>
42) SLDAPICUST – SLD API customizing. This allows the communication between the integration engine and SLD to get system details at runtime.
43) RZ70 – SLD administration.
44) SLDHTML – Start SLD GUI in a browser.

Alerts related:
45) ALRTCATDEF_SEL – Define alert category.
46) ALRTCATDEF – Edit alert category.

Note: We should have authorization of role SAP_SI_ADMINISTRATOR. We must enter the following:

- *Receiver of alert*
- *Title of alert*
- *Text of alert, including container variables that are filled at runtime*
- *Follow up activity*

47) ALRTDISP – Display alerts.
48) ALRTINBOX – Alert inbox.
49) ALRTPERS – Personalize alert delivery.
50) ALRTPROC – Process alerts.
51) ALRTSUBSCR – Subscribe to alert categories.

INTRODUCTORY QUESTIONS

Question 1: BAPI not found when creating Models

When I create a model in NetWeaver, I can find all the BAPIs that are in the system except the ones I've created.

Can you give me an idea where to find my BAPI?

A: You need to check "Remote-enabled module", which is located in the attributes for your BAPI/RFC.

Question 2: Transporting XI objects

IIow do you transport an XI object like the repository or directory to the QA system?

A: You can transport XI objects either by CMS or by file export.

To accomplish the transport, go to "Tools", then "Export objects" and it will be exported as ".tpz" file. You can place the same in the repository_server/import and directory_server/import directory and import it from your QA system.

There is web blog in SDN, which you can visit for more details concerning transporting objects.

Question 3: File not deleted after successful execution

I deleted a file to an IDOC scenario in RWB. After a successful processing, the file was not deleted from the location. This error was displayed:

```
"Could not delete file 'F:\XIShared\test\1.XML' after
processing".
```

How can I prevent this kind of error from appearing again?

A: You will need to access the properties/permissions for the file you processed. Check that the file is not "read only" in the folder. A "read only" property means that the file cannot be deleted, so in order to delete the file you would have to change the setting if possible.

Question 4: Messages in HTML Format

I am using a scenario JDBC to file. I don't want the receiver in file format, but in HTML format instead. Also, if I use JDBC to RFC scenario, instead of having the format in RFC, can I have the file in some other format, for example HTML?

A: No. RFC's have to use XML. Remember that your RFC call is going to invoke a function module into an R/3 system and the R/3 system needs to understand the information you are passing. XI only uses and understands XML as its communicating language/medium.

But when sending data outside XI to another application, you can convert this XML payload into any format you want by using adapter modules, content conversion, etc.

Question 5: Mail Package

I am using the Mail Package detailed in a "weblog" to send emails. I want to attach the payload to the email.

Is this possible?

A: Yes it is. You need to use XSLT mapping for this to work.

Question 6: Changing the Name of Datatype

I created a Datatype and saved it. I now need to change the name of the Datatype but it will not allow me to change the name.

Is there a way I can change the name of the Datatype?

A: It is not possible to directly change the name of a datatype.

If you want to preserve the data, then first make a copy of the datatype, and then give the name you want to the copy. Save the copy, and then delete the original data type. You have now essentially "renamed" the datatype.

Question 7: File to File

Can you please explain the steps required for completing "File Inbound" and "Outbound" in a local machine (file read from local directory and write into local directory)?

A: You will need to do a lot of reading to understand the topic you are asking. I have made an outline as follows:

Communication channel:

Assigning Communication Channels

Communication Channel

Configuring the Sender File/FTP Adapter

Configuring the Receiver File/FTP Adapter

Receiver agreement:

Receiver Agreement

Creating a Receiver Agreement

Sender agreement:

Sender Agreement

Creating a Sender Agreement

INSTALLATION, AUTHORIZATION, & CONNECTION ISSUES

Question 8: Business Transaction Codes

I was using 'we19' to test an inbound IDoc mbgmcr02. I got the message "status 51 qty and/or delivery completed ind or final issue ind are missing". I have the quantity filled in. I need the delivery completed "ind" or final issue "ind" filled in.

On the e1BP2017_gm_code, I use a code 02.

Can you give me the rundown on the valid codes to use here and what they mean?

A: Here is a list of Business Transactions/Events codes.

- GM_Code 01: Goods receipt for purchase order
- GM_Code 02: Goods receipt for production order
- GM_Code 03: Goods issue
- GM_Code 04: Transfer posting
- GM_Code 05: Other goods receipts
- GM_Code 06: Reversal of goods movements
- GM_Code 07: Subsequent adjustment to a subcontract order

Question 9: Problems while deploying Java Proxy

We generated Java proxy of our interface and tried to deploy the same into our WAS 6.4 using NetWeaver Dev Studio.

We successfully created ".ear" file. But while deploying the file, it gave the following error:

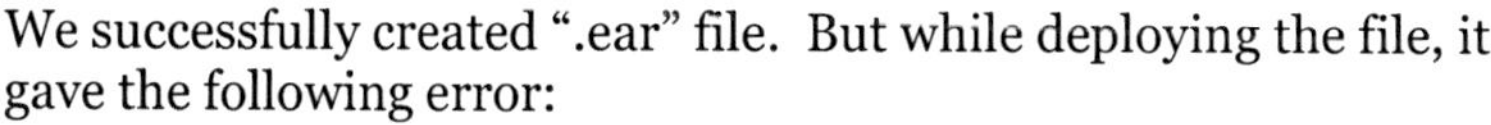

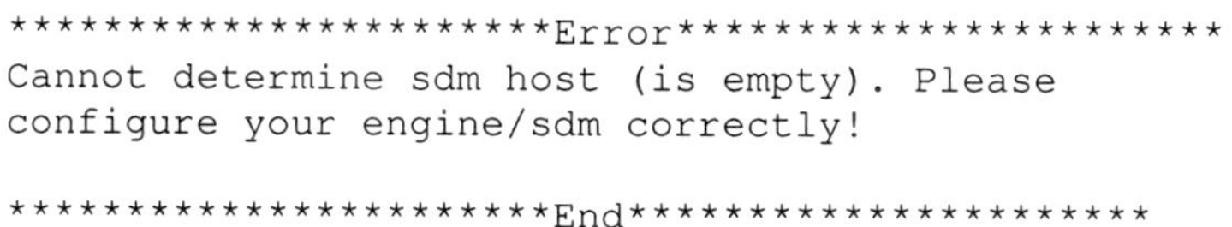

```
*********************Error*********************
Cannot determine sdm host (is empty). Please
configure your engine/sdm correctly!


*********************End*********************
```

The J2EE engine of XI server is configured with NWDS. Also according to the documentation of SAP, we manually restarted the SDM using 'startserver.bat' but still the problem persists.

Can you help us solve this problem?

A: Yes. Make sure that you have given message to the server port (3600) and not to the J2EE port (50000).

Instead of using NWDS, use SDM directly and deploy the ".ear". The ".ear" file will be there in your workspace folder when you need to use it. In your XI server, search for "RemoteGui.bat", then double click on it click on deployment, then choose your ".ear", then deploy.

Question 10: 'functiontemplate' from repository was <null>

We have a simple R/3 (RFC) to XI to R/3 (RFC) scenario that is currently working. After some time we decided to add another RFC, so we made the necessary work in IR and ID under the existing namespace and scenario respectively. We created the RFCs in every backend doing the same steps that we did for the existing RFCs that are currently working.

When we sent the message using the new RFCs in SXMB_MONI, we encountered the error:

```
com.sap.aii.af.ra.ms.api.DeliveryException: error
while processing message to remote
system:com.sap.aii.af.rfc.core.client.RfcClientExcept
ion: functiontemplate from repository was <null>
```

We tried to send the payload in the RWB and comparing the new RFC with the one that is working in SXMB_MONI. The difference is that the new RFC shows no response. It just appears in the payload of the receiver but no acknowledgment is shown. On the contrary, the RFC that is working shows acknowledgment:

```
"Legacy system to which acknowledgment message is to
be sent is missing in hoplist (with wasread=false)";
```

So far, this is the only difference that we have noticed. We have checked the Interface Mappings and Message Mappings and everything looks like the RFC that works.

We have shutdown java and repeated the steps re-importing the RFCs even with other names, and the error is the same.

Can you help us solve this?

A: Yes. You need to only check your RFC Communication Channel. Make sure it is working correctly.

Question 11: ExchangeProfile Problem

I installed NW04 (ABAP+J2EE) and XI. On page 33 of XI post installation, I created a user XISUPER in ABAP system and rebooted J2EE Server.

I did not find the XISUPER in the J2EE instance. Did I do something wrong here or is there any additional steps needed to be done apart from what document says? As a result, I was not able to do an import of ExchangeProfile. I search Google.com and SDN and found that I could use J2EE_ADMIN, but when I tried to do so, I received the following error "You are not authorized to view the requested resource".

My J2ee_admin has Administrator role and for group I have Authenticated Users, Everyone, SAP_J2EE_ADMIN.

Can you give any solution/s to this problem?

A: Two things are important for J2EE users in regards to XI.

1. During installation of J2EE you should select the XI UME option; otherwise users are stored separately in ABAP and J2EE.
2. The UME client must be the correct one as described on page 16 in the XI Install guide.

Reinstall the java system. At the point where it asks for production client, the value should match with the client that you want to use as an Integration server. 000 is the original value; you should match it with the client's. For example, if you called the client 100, then production client should also be 100. Any mismatch will result into the problem you are facing.

Question 12: XI Installation Problems

Our XI installation failed during the phase deploying
SAPXIAF04_1.SCA. The displayed error message in SDM:

```
Jul 14, 2006 12:35:07... Error: Aborted: development
component
'com.sap.aii.adapter.jms.app'/'sap.com'/'SAP
AG'/'7.0004.20050713150837.0000':
Caught exception while checking the login credentials
for SAP J2EE Engine. Check whether the SAP J2EE
Engine is up and running.
com.sap.engine.deploy.manager.DeployManagerException:
ERROR: Cannot connect to Host: [cixid] with user
name: [J2EE_ADMIN]
Check your login information.
Exception is:
com.sap.engine.services.jndi.persistent.exceptions.Na
mingException: Exception while trying to get
InitialContext. [Root exception is
com.sap.engine.services.security.exceptions.BaseLogin
Exception: Cannot create new RemoteLoginContext
instance.]
(message ID:
com.sap.sdm.serverext.servertype.inqmy.extern.EngineA
pplOnlineDeployerImpl.checkLoginCredentials.DMEXC)
```

I have checked the login name and password is ok. There is an
OSS note 756084 section 4 suggesting the problem was due to
TicketLoginModule. I don't think we have changed any login
modules, as it is an installation. We also couldn't start the VA.

Do you have any suggestion or solution for this problem?

A: You can solve the problem by doing the following:

Configtool -> dispatcher -> Service -> P4.

For 'bindhost' option, you will need to enter your CI instance
hostname/ipaddress (default is 0.0.0.0).

Question 13: XI Install Error

I was attempting to install XI on a MSCS cluster Environment - Windows Server 2003 Enterprise Edition, running Oracle 9.2.0.6. I have installed our Dev, QA and Production systems successfully. I also installed Oracle, OraFS, ABAP+Java on MSCS Cluster, and was trying to install XI Component.

When SAP installer was running, I got the following error message after I entered the Domain, userid and password:

```
INFO 2006-03-08 15:46:29
Installation start: Wednesday, 08 March 2006,
15:46:25; installation
directory: C:\sapinstall\XI; product to be installed:
SAP NetWeaver '04
Support Release 1> NetWeaver Components Running on
Java> XI Components>
Exchange Infrastructure Installation

WARNING 2006 03 08 15:46:46
The step storeSidadmPassword with step key
ExchangeInfrastructure|ind|ind|ind|ind|ind|0|Gener
icAskJavahomeAndPasswords|ind|ind|ind|ind|ind|0|st
oreSidadmPassword was executed with status
ERROR.

WARNING 2006-03-08 15:46:52
An error occurred during the installation.
```

The password for <SID>adm has the "@" sign in, and I wonder if this caused the error.

Is there a solution for this?

A: Yes. You need to do the following.

```
In the control.xml, change the line:
WindowsDomain = gui.getInputValue(
"fld_WindowsDomain" );
To
WindowsDomain = context.get("WindowsDomain");
Continue installation.
```

Question 14: FTP Connection Error

I tried to run the File to IDoc scenario. In this case I used FTP as sender channel. During execution in the adapter monitor I received the following error:

```
Sender Adapter v1028 for Party '', Service 'FILE_BS':
Configured at 12:45:07 2006-07-06
Processing Error: Error connecting to ftp server
'192.168.13.9': com.sap.aii.adapter.file.ftp.FTPEx:
/Inetpub/ftproot: The system cannot find the path
specified.
last retry interval started 12:45:07 2006-07-06
length 60,000 secs
```

Can you tell me what caused the error?

I did the configuration everywhere and I have given everyone permission. I kept the directory in a shared folder. I am able to access the directory from XI server.

Can you tell if any other configuration is missing?

Folder path : /Inetpub/ftproot
file name : xiinput.txt

A: You need to first do a cross check on the path >> Folder path : /Inetpub/ftproot

Then check if you have assigned read/write rights to the FTP folder.

Note that if your ftproot is the FTP folder, then / is your root folder in XI adapter so if you have a folder input in ftproot, in your CC you will specify:

folder : /input

And not:

ftproot/input

Question 15: XI Lost Connection to J2EE

Sometimes, the XI system seems to lose connection to the J2EE server, and the RFC connections AI_DIRECTORY_JCOSERVER, AI_RUNTIME_JCOSERVER, etc. stops working, and then all messages fail.

Logs in dev_jcontrol show errors like:

```
[Thr 3596] Thu Sep 15 18:34:24 2005
[Thr 3596] ***LOG Q0I=> NiPRead: recv (10054:
WSAECONNRESET: Connection reset by peer) [ninti.c
785]
[Thr 3596] *** ERROR => MsINiRead: NiBufReceive
failed (NIECONN_BROKEN) [msxxi.c 2488]
[Thr 3596] *** ERROR => MsIReadFromHdl: NiRead
(rc=NIECONN_BROKEN) [msxxi.c 1652]
[Thr 3596] ***LOG Q0I=> NiPConnect2: SiPeekPendConn
(10065: WSAEHOSTUNREACH: No route to host)
[nixxi_r.cpp 8605]
[Thr 3596] *** ERROR => MsIAttachEx: NiBufConnect to
sapserver4/3601 failed (rc=NIECONN_REFUSED) [msxxi.c
633]
[Thr 3596] *** WARNING => Can't reconnect to message
server (sapserver4/3601) [rc = -100]-> reconnect
[jcntrms.c 296]
[Thr 6612] ***LOG Q0I=> NiPRead: recv (10054:
WSAECONNRESET: Connection reset by peer) [ninti.c
785]

[Thr 3596] Thu Sep 15 18:34:29 2005
[Thr 3596] *** ERROR => MsIAttachEx: NiBufConnect to
sapserver4/3601 failed (rc=NIECONN_REFUSED) [msxxi.c
633]
[Thr 3596] *** WARNING => Can't reconnect to message
server (sapserver4/3601) [rc = -100]-> reconnect
[jcntrms.c 296]
```

Do you have any suggestions concerning this problem?

A: I see this issue often in our XI systems. To date, there is only one solution: restart the JCos. We have not been able to determine why these JCos lose their registration in the gateway,it occasionally occurs.

The next time it happens, go to tcode SMGW and go to "Logged on clients". You should see the above-mentioned RFC's logged onto the gateway. If you don't see them, then open the VA on the XI server to stop then start each affected JCo. Once it is restarted, check the gateway again to see if they have registered. Your system will be good to go without restarting the entire J2EE engine.

Question 16: JCo Connection Parameters and Migration through Dev/QA/Prod

I know how to open up from within XI a JCo connection to an SAP client.

How do you determine what SAP client to connect to and how to migrate that along when you move the XI development from Dev to QA to Prod?

A: You will need to manage with a "prop file". Just give it the same name on the three systems (Dev, QA, and Production). Keep it in a separate 'Imported Archive' (separate java package as well), and load it from java as resource. You can do this in 1 SWCV and then have others base themselves off of that one so you only have to do it once.

If you cannot upload objects directly into QA and Production, a "prop file" on the "filesystem" is better. Choose a suitable location existing on the three systems.

When using the Lookup API with RFC/JCo, you still need the name of the "Service without Pary". You have to put this name in a properties file on the "filesystem" of the XI server. The file will have the same name (but different contents) on Dev, QA and Production.

You can also use the SAP XI value mapping to store configuration parameters.

Question 17: sm58 - Name or Password is Incorrect

I have encountered a problem. After the configuration of an IDoc to File, I am facing an error "sm58" after successfully sending an IDoc with "we19".

Status text indicated: `"Name or password is incorrect. Please re-enter".`

After retrying, I've got a new error message:

`"User is locked. Please notify the person responsible".`

How do I sort this out?

A: You need to check your SM59 connection (Target system column in SM58). There is most probably a userid/password defined that is incorrect. You have to unlock the user in the target system.

Be careful. Normally, when you try to access your SAP systems with an invalid user id / password more than 3 times, the user gets locked. You will have to ask your admin to unlock the user and then make your remote log on test in Sm 59.

Cross check first with these steps in what you have done so far.

While doing an IDoc to XI to File scenario, take note of the following points:

1. You don't need a DT, MT or a message interface for the IDoc as it itself acts as the Message Interface.
2. You import the IDoc and use the same in your mapping.
3. In this configuration, note that you don't have a sender agreement as you don't have a sender IDoc adapter.

If it is that you wanted to send an IDoc from XI (File to IDoc), then in this case:

Points 1 and 2 will remain, but the 3rd will not. You will need a sender agreement for the file and a receiver agreement for the IDoc.

IDoc to File scenario reference:

https://www.sdn.sap.com/irj/sdn/weblogs?blog=/pub/wlg/1819

Configurations in R/3 side:

1. SM 59 (RFC destinations)

    Create a RFC destination on the XI server. The connection type should be R/3 connection. The target host needs to be the XI server.

2. WE 21 (Ports in IDoc processing)

    Create a transactional port. Provide the RFC destination created in this.

3. BD 54

    Create a logical system.

4. WE 20 (Partner Profiles)

    a. Create a new partner profile under partner type LS.

    b. Assign the message type in outbound parameters.

    c. Open the message type (Dbl click) and configure the receiver port to the port created.

XI Server Configurations:

1. SM59 (RFC destination)

    Configure the RFC destination specific to the R/3 system.

2. IDX1 (Port maintenance in IDoc Adapter)

Create a port and provide the RFC destination.

TESTING:

WE19 for pushing the IDoc in XI through trfc port.

To be able to trigger your IDOC from the SAP ISU system, you will have to set the partner profile in "we20". Select your Business System (mostly under Logical system) and then create outbound entries for whichever IDoc you want to trigger.

You define your basic type also in your partner profile settings. Please go thru the following links to get a better idea about partner profile:

http://help.sap.com/saphelp_nw04/helpdata/en/dc/6b833243d711d1893e0000e8323c4f/frameset.htm

http://help.sap.com/saphelp_nw04/helpdata/en/dc/6b7cd343d711d1893e0000e8323c4f/frameset.htm

http://help.sap.com/saphelp_nw04/helpdata/en/32/692037b1f10709e10000009b38f839/content.htm

http://help.sap.com/saphelp_nw04/helpdata/en/5e/b8f8bf356dc84096e4fedc2cd71426/frameset.htm

I would suggest that you go through these blogs if any more issues arise.

https://weblogs.sdn.sap.com/pub/wlg/1439

https://weblogs.sdn.sap.com/pub/wlg/1843

Question 18: "You are not authorized to view the requested resource in SLD"

After logging into SXMB_IFR, I tried to get some SLD components but I instead got the "You are not authorized to view the requested resource in SLD" message.

What do I need to do to get into SLD?

A: You will need to check the role or level of authorization you have.

SAP_SLD_ADMINISTRATOR

Or

SAP_SLD_CONFIGURATOR

Or

SAP_XI_CONFIGURATOR

Or

SAP_XI_CONTENT_ORGANIZER

For a complete definition of roles and level of authorization, check out the following link.

http://help.sap.com/saphelp_nw04/helpdata/en/c4/51104159e cef23e10000000a155106/content.htm

Question 19: RWB Error during Message Monitoring

I received the following error during Message monitoring:

```
"User XIRWBUSER has no RFC authorization for function
group HTTPTREE, error key: RFC_ERROR_SYSTEM_FAILURE"
```

What can this mean and how do I fix it?

A: First, check if your XIRWBUSER has its standard roles.

SAP_XI_RWB_SERV_USER
SAP_XI_RWB_SERV_USER_MAIN

Normally the mentioned roles should be sufficient.

Another key is the SP level of your XI system. After a new SP
level, XI will request more authorizations that have not been
included in the standard role so far. You will need to open up an
OSS message at SAP.

The standard role has been extended with a new SP but the
according profile has not been regenerated, so you will also need
to carry out a mass generation of all profiles for SAP_XI roles
and after that a user comparison.

Question 20: Websphere MQ Problem

I have a problem with Websphere MQ Sender adapter. I know that there are messages are in the queue, but XI doesn't get them. I have checked everything in the adapter engine and integration engine.

There are no errors and all lights are green. There is no payload.

Can I make the adapter work?

A: Yes. You need to reset your communication channel. Deactivate and activate it again.

Question 21: Reassigning Change List to a Different User

One user in our system has changed SWCV, but did not activate the change list. The system pops out the message saying:

"If necessary, you can reassign the other user's change list to yourself"

How do I find what the system requires?

A: Open the Integration Builder Web Start application and go to the "change list" tab. Select the user that has changed the SWCV and press "Display". You can now assign the change list to yours if you right-click on it and press "OK".

Question 22: Setting up HTTPS

We added an SSL certificate to our XI server. We are struggling our way through the documentation for the steps to exchange messages via HTTPS.

How do I set the adapter to use HTTPS in the integration directory?

I only see HTTP 1.0 in the options for protocol while trying to setup the HTTP adapter settings.

The external party is the receiver of messages from us. During testing, no security was in place so we tried sending to a URL using the HTTP adapter. Now, HTTPS protocol must be used. However, for the HTTP adapter type, HTTPS protocol is not a drop down option.

Does that mean I have to use adapter type "XI" to send to a URL via HTTPS?

A: You need to do the following to fix your problem.

In the communication channel select the following:

- Transport protocol : HTTP1.0
- Addressing Type : HTTP Destination
- HTTP Destination: your ABAP RFC (type G)

In your RFC destination, you need to specify the URL and the certificate to use to connect to your server.

ADAPTER & ADAPTER ENGINE FAQ

Question 23: Adapter Engine

I need to change the host name of the adapter engine that is showing up in RWB under integration server.

How do I accomplish this?

A: The host name displayed in RWB is simply XI server's host name. If you change server host name, it will reflect there.

Visit the following link for more details:

http://help.sap.com/saphelp_nw04/helpdata/en/ea/fo284od89 d185de10000000a1550bo/frameset.htm

Question 24: Adapter Engine not found in ID

I just installed my system with XI3.0 SP12 and this adapter engine problem occurred while developing my first integration scenario, IDoc - File.

Adapter Engine for File adapter is not available to select from drop down while configuring CC.

An SLDCHECK gave this result:

```
'no corresponding biz system found for xi system' ==>
check and maintain the SLD content for the current
system

EXCHANGE_PROFILE_GET_PARAMETER function:
returned exception code 2
Access to the XI profile is currently disrupted'
```

What could have caused this problem? Can you help me solve this?

A: Given that this is a new installation, check that the XI Content for SAP Basis 6.40 (SP12 since that's what your XI system is on) has been imported into the 'Integration Repository'. This is one of the post-installation steps defined in the Install Guide. Within this step is the adapter metadata for all the delivered adapters. Without following this step completely, this problem, and many others, will arise.

Also, check that you have adequately carried out all the post-installation steps of the install guide. It is critical that this be done before moving on to design and configuration of scenarios.

Question 25: *Adapter Engine Errors*

This is a JDBC receiver scenario.

A message that fails with a 'System Error in Adapter Engine' does not raise alerts but 'Integration engine - system error' messages raises alerts.

What I mean is in message monitoring - choosing Integration Server and displaying the messages (messages with status system error and engine to adapter engine) does not raise alerts.

Can you give a clarification concerning this matter?

A: If you are on:

SP12 - There is no way for you to raise alerts.

SP13 - You can configure CCMS to raise alerts for Adapter Engine.

SP14 on wards - You have the option of specifying adapter alert rules.

Alert configuration may sometimes cause some problems. With the steps provided in the link below you can quickly find out what might be the reason.

Question 26: J2SE Adapter Engine / JMS Adapter

We need to connect to MQ Series 5.3 (Websphere MQ) from the XI (3.0 SP16) box.

Do J2SE adapter engine need to be enabled/configured in order to use JMS Adapter? Can't we use J2EE JMSAdapter instead of J2SE JMS Adapter? Where can I download the JMS Adapter libraries, for installation?

Ours is UNIX-based installation.

I have gone thru the thread below and the SAP Note: 747601 that talks about J2EE JMSAdapter MQSeries libraries.

A: Standard JMS adapter comes with XI. When you are trying to connect to external systems like "MQ" or "Sonic", you need to get the "client" files from the vendor, and then you need to deploy the same in your XI.

You can download the libraries from the market place.

Question 27: Ping Error in RWB for J2SE Adapter Engine

We have several external J2SE adapter engines and they function great other than from a monitoring perspective. In RWB "Ping Status", I'm getting the following:

HTTP request failed. Error code: "401". Error message: "Authorization Required"

Do you have any idea what's causing this?

A: You will need to check the following:

1. If user: XIRWBUSER is not locked in R/3
2. If you got a correct password in the XI exchange profile:
   a. com.sap.aii.rwb.serviceuser.name
   b. com.sap.aii.rwb.serviceuser.pwd
   c. com.sap.aii.rwb.serviceuser.language

Question 28: RFC Adapter Problem: Adapter Engine Field Blank

I want to invoke a BAPI defined on an R/3 system. I am trying to create a RFC Adapter in the Integration Directory by creating a communication channel.

I am facing a problem when I define the Adapter Type as RFC; the Adapter Engine dropdown list is blank and it does not contain any entries.

On passing a document through XI, I can see the following error in the monitor:

```
<SAP:Code
area="INTERNAL">ADAPTER_NAME_INVALID</SAP:Code>
<SAP:P1>RFC</SAP:P1>
<SAP:P2>PLSRV_CALL_ADAPTER</SAP:P2>
<SAP:P3 />
<SAP:P4 />
<SAP:AdditionalText />
<SAP:ApplicationFaultMessage namespace="" />
<SAP:Stack>Unknown receiver adapter (name =
RFC)</SAP:Stack>
```

What do I need to configure on the XI and R/3 side?

The following entries appear in the SLD for content maintenance, class XI Integration Server. My machine name is netweaver and SID is NW4.

```
XI Contained Integration Server
GroupComponent: XI Domain Domain netweaver
XI Integration Server Logical Identity
SameElement: Business System NW4
```

A: Your problem is caused by an omission in SLD that occurred when the installation was done. Your SLD is missing a third entry:

```
"XI Sub-System viewed application system";
```

After you add this, you need to restart the SLD server from SLD administration page.

If you are still not getting the populated adapter engine list, you will need to configure your business and technical systems correctly, make the necessary associations, and then you will be able to see the Integration Server in the RFC adapter drop down.

Question 29: Error in Adapter Engine

I installed XI 3.0 SP9 with jre 1.4.2-08. When I selected the
'Adapter type' as File in 'Sender' mode while configuring the
scenario FILE-IDoc by following the weblog in the Integration
directory, I did not get the values for Adapter Engine
(Integration Server), which is mandatory. But when I selected
IDoc, XI adapter types, I was able to get Integration Server.

I checked in the Runtime workbench, Adapter Monitoring, and
there I saw an error in SLD access saying that JPR configuration
is not done. I concluded that the problem is with the
configuration of Adapter Engine.

How can I solve this problem?

A: You need to create a business system BS_JPR for Web AS
Java type. You will see the JPR turning green. This is not
related to the integration directory in your case.

The default adapter engine is Integration Server. There could be
more if you have installed PCK or another XI instance.

You will have to use the Integration Server Adapter Engine.

You will also need to restart your XI server after the above steps.

Question 30: Decentralized Adapter Engine

We have installed an XI landscape (XID, XIQ, and XIP) on UNIX along with a single decentralized Adapter Engine on Windows (XD1) that is currently configured for use with our XID system. We would like to also use this same decentralized Adapter Engine with our XIQ system. However, when we export a communication channel from XID (configured to use the decentralized adapter engine af.XID.calxid1 and subsequently import the communication channel into XIQ), the decentralized Adapter engine that was configured in XID (af.XD1.calxid1) was replaced with "Integration Server" (Default) in the Communication Channel configuration in XIQ. The pull down to choose an adapter engine shows only the (Default) Integration server as an available choice. Currently, XID and XIQ are using the same SLD and the decentralized adapter engine (af.XD1.calxid1) is identified there. I have been unable to determine how to use the decentralized adapter engine with our XIQ system.

Is it possible to have multiple XI systems using the same decentralized Adapter Engine? And if it is possible, how do you configure the second XI system (XIQ) to use the decentralized adapter engine?

A: No, it is not possible to have multiple XI systems use the same decentralized Adapter Engine. A decentralized Adapter Engine can only be attached to a single Integration Server. The best solution is to install a decentralized Adapter Engine for every XI system you want to use.

Question 31: Unable to Find any Adapter Engines

I encountered a problem when attempting to execute a scenario. An xml-file is read from a drive by the XI system. XI read the values. Another xml-file containing some parts of this info was written to another location. I saw that the file was read and removed.

However, when I checked the monitoring, I found following error message:

```
<SAP:Error
xmlns:SAP="http://sap.com/xi/XI/Message/30"
xmlns:SOAP="http://schemas.xmlsoap.org/soap/envelope/
" SOAP:mustUnderstand="">
<SAP:Category>XIServer</SAP:Category>
<SAP:Code
area="INTERNAL">AE_DETAILS_GET_ERROR</SAP:Code>
<SAP:P1>af.cx1.cernum05\cx1</SAP:P1>
<SAP:P2 />
<SAP:P3 />
<SAP:P4 />
<SAP:AdditionalText>Exception in SLD client:
AbapSLDRequestHandler.exe: Unable to find any Adapter
Engines</SAP:AdditionalText>
<SAP:ApplicationFaultMessage namespace="" />
<SAP:Stack>Error when reading the access data (URL,
user, password) for the Adapter Engine
af.cx1.cernum05\cx1</SAP:Stack>
<SAP:Retry>M</SAP:Retry>
</SAP:Error>
```

Is a configuration missing? Are there things that I forgot to check out? We are running XI3.0 SP9.

A: You need to execute transaction SE37 and test the function module SAI_AE_DETAILS_GET. Enter your AE_NAME af.<hostname>.<sysid> and execute.

You also need to run an SLDCHECK and check whether your exchange profile parameter checks are successful. The last one Calling function EXCHANGE_PROFILE_GET_PARAMETER.

If these are correct, check that your
com.sap.aii.adapterframework.serviceuser.name and
com.sap.aii.adapterframework.serviceuser.pwd are correct.

If these are correct, check whether the user id is locked.

In addition, check whether you are using the SLD that is on your
XI server or you are pointing to a different SLD.

Question 32: File Adapter Command

I am running a command after a message processing is complete.
If the UNIX command fails, is there a way to have that show up
as a failure in SXMB_MONI?

A: You will not see any status in SXMB_MONI, since the
message has been sent successfully to the file adapter.

However, in RWB, for adapter message monitoring, there will be
a warning indicating the command has failed.

If you want to debug because you cannot see any status in
SXMB_MONI, visit:

Question 33: Receiver Mail Adapter

I tried to configure an HTTP to XI to mail adapter. I used my company's mail address for this. I don't get any errors in SXMB_MONI and RWB, but the mail is not delivered to my inbox. I checked the Message monitoring.

The detailed audit log shows:

```
2006-08-29 14:46:23 Success output 1156842983828 The
message was successfully received by the messaging
system. Profile: XI URL:
http://sap1:50000/MessagingSystem/receive/AFW/XI
2006-08-29 14:46:23 Success output 1156842983843
Using connection AFW. Trying to put the message into
the receive queue.
2006-08-29 14:46:23 Success
SAPEngine_Application_Thread[impl:3]_11 1156842983875
The message was successfully retrieved from the
receive queue.
2006-08-29 14:46:23 Success
SAPEngine_Application_Thread[impl:3]_11 1156842983937
The message status set to DLNG.
2006-08-29 14:46:23 Success
SAPEngine_Application_Thread[impl:3]_11 1156842983968
Delivering to channel: CC_MailTest
2006-08-29 14:46:24 Success
SAPEngine_Application_Thread[impl:3]_11 1156842984000
Mail: message entering the adapter
2006-08-29 14:46:44 Error
SAPEngine_Application_Thread[impl:3]_11 1156843004953
Exception caught by adapter framework: Failed to call
the endpoint
2006-08-29 14:46:44 Error
SAPEngine_Application_Thread[impl:3]_11 1156843004953
Delivery of the message to the application using
connection AFW failed, due to: Failed to call the
endpoint.
2006-08-29 14:46:44 Success
SAPEngine_Application_Thread[impl:3]_11 1156843004984
The asynchronous message was successfully scheduled
to be delivered at Tue Aug 29 14:51:44 GMT+05:30
2006.
2006-08-29 14:46:45 Success
SAPEngine_Application_Thread[impl:3]_11 1156843005000
The message status set to WAIT.
```

The parameters of the mail adapter are:

Transport Protocol : SMTP
Message Protocol : XIALL
Adapter Engine : Integration Server

url : smtp://<server name>.caritor.com
user : jaishankar
password : ******

From : jaishankar.ramakrishnan@caritor.com
To : jaishankar.ramakrishnan@caritor.com
Subject : test mail from XI

I think these parameters are correct.

Why can't the mail get delivered to my inbox?

A: Yes, your parameters seem to be correct. The only thing you can do is to ask your "basis people" if your XI server has access to the company mail server (opened ports, etc.) Also check with your office email admin team whether the SMTP address entered is correct or not.

Question 34: Adapter Monitor Message

In a file to file to scenario, I got the following message in Adapter monitor:

"Receiver Adapter v1027 for Party ", Service 'YAMAHA_BS':
Configured at 18:31:43 2008-10-17
Up and running - no message processing until now"

What exactly is this error?

A: This is not an error message.

"Up and running - no message processing until now";

Your receiver file adapter is ready to poll the data as it has been configured successfully. It means that XI receiver adapter has not processed any messages until now. If the sender has picked the file, check it in SXMB_MONI, there might be some error.

Question 35: Setting the Username & Password for the Plain HTTP Adapter

When I passed a HTTP request into the integration engine's plain_http adapter url, I was required to give a username and a password for authentication.

Is it possible to set this username and password globally somewhere?

This is to avoid the username and password to be given again and again for each message. The requirement is like all http messages from our partners will be routed through a proxy in the DMZ that would have an authentication and we do not want the XI user credentials to be given repeatedly.

A: You need to use SICF, then sap/xi/adapter_plain, then change button. Enter client, username, password, and language.

If you want to just test the http adapter use this code:

```html
<html>

<script type="text/javascript">;
<!--
function button1_onclick() {
var result = "Result: ";
var payload = "<?xml version=\"1.0\" encoding=\"UTF-8\" ?>";
// escape "http://"
var senderNamespace =
escape(document.MessageParameters.SenderNamespace.val
ue);

var reqString = "http://"
reqString = reqString +
document.MessageParameters.Server.value+":";
reqString = reqString +
document.MessageParameters.Port.value +
"/sap/xi/adapter_plain?";
reqString = reqString + "namespace=" +
senderNamespace;
reqString = reqString + "&interface=" +
document.MessageParameters.SenderInterface.value;
reqString = reqString + "&service=" +
```

```
document.MessageParameters.SenderService.value;
reqString = reqString + "&party=" +
document.MessageParameters.SenderParty.value;
reqString = reqString + "&agency=" +
document.MessageParameters.SenderAgency.value;
reqString = reqString + "&scheme=" +
document.MessageParameters.SenderScheme.value;
reqString = reqString + "&QOS=" +
document.MessageParameters.qos.value;

reqString = reqString + "&queueid=httpclient";

reqString = reqString + "&sap-user=" +
document.MessageParameters.username.value;
reqString = reqString + "&sap-password=" +
document.MessageParameters.password.value;
reqString = reqString + "&sap-client=" +
document.MessageParameters.Client.value
reqString = reqString + "&sap-language=EN";
var xhttp = new ActiveXObject("msxml2.xmlhttp");

for (var i=0;
i<document.MessageParameters.retry.value; i++) {

  xhttp.open ("POST", reqString, false);
 document.MessageParameters.URL.value=reqString;

  if (document.MessageParameters.Source[0].checked ==
true) {
    payload = "<?xml version=\"1.0\" encoding=\"UTF-
8\" ?> "+ document.MessageParameters.xmlData.value;
    xhttp.send (payload);
  } else{
    var xmlDoc = new
ActiveXObject("microsoft.xmldom");
    xmlDoc.async=false;
    xmlDoc.load
(document.MessageParameters.xmlFile.value);
    xhttp.send (xmlDoc);
  }
result = result + "\nhttp-Status:  " + xhttp.status +
" " + xhttp.statusText + " \nPayload:\n" +
xhttp.responseText;

xhttp.close;
document.MessageParameters.response.value=result;
}


}
```

```
//-->
</script>
<head></head>

<body>

<h3>Client Http Adapter </h3>
<form name="MessageParameters">
<table border="1" cellpadding="0" cellspacing="0"
style="border-collapse: collapse"
bordercolor="#111111" width="100%">
<h4>Header</h4>
<tbody>
<tr>
<td width="10%"><label>Server Host</label> </td>
<td width="22%">

<!-- Change server and port here -->

<input type="text" id="host" name="Server"
value="YourServer" size="20" /> </td>
<td width="10%"><label>Server Port</label> </td>
<td width="22%"><input type="text" id="port"
name="Port" value="8000" size="10" /> </td>
</tr>
<tr>
<td width="10%">Client</td>
<td width="22%">

<!-- Change client here -->

<input type="text" id="client" name="Client"
value="100" size="3" /></td>
<td width="10%"> </td>
<td width="22%"> </td>
</tr>
<tr>
<td width="10%"><label>Sender Service</label> </td>
<td width="22%">

<!-- Change sender service here -->

<input type="text" id="senderService"
name="SenderService" value="TravelAgencyCS" size="40"
/> </td>
<td width="10%">Quality of Service</td>
<td width="22%">
        <select size="1" name="qos">
        <option value="BE">Best Effort
```

```html
(synchronous)</option>
      <option value="EO" selected>Exactly Once
(asynchronous)</option>
      <option value="EOIO">Exactly Once in
Order</option>
      </select>
</td>
</tr>
<tr>
<td width="10%"><label>Sender Interface</label> </td>

<!-- Change sender interface name here -->

<td width="22%"><input type="text"
id="senderInterface"
name="SenderInterface" value="BookingOrdersOut"
size="40" /> </td>
<td width="10%"><label>Sender Namespace</label> </td>
<td width="22%">

<!-- Change sender interface namespace  here -->

<input type="text" id="senderNamespace"
name="SenderNamespace"
value="http://sap.com/xi/rkt/CaseStudy/group99"
size="40" /></td>
</tr>
</tbody>
</table>
<br>
<table border="1" cellpadding="0" cellspacing="0"
style="border-collapse: collapse"
bordercolor="#111111" width="100%">
<h4>Optional Parameters</h4>
<tbody>
<tr>
<td width="10%">Sender Party</td>
<td width="22%"><input type="text" id="senderParty"
name="SenderParty" size="40" /></td>
</tr>
<tr>
<td width="10%">Sender Agency</td>
<td width="22%"><input type="text" id="senderAgency"
name="SenderAgency" size="40" /></td>
<td width="10%">Sender Scheme</td>
<td width="22%"><input type="text" id="senderScheme"
name="SenderScheme" size="40" /></td>
</tr>
```

```
 <TR>
   <TD width="10%">Username</TD>

<!-- Change user name here -->

    <TD width="22%"><INPUT id=username size=40
value=xiappluser name=username></TD>
    <TD width="10%">Password</TD>
    <TD width="22%"><INPUT id=password type=password
size=40  name=password></TD></TR>
  <TR>
    <TD width="10%">Retry</TD>
    <TD width="22%"><INPUT id=retry type=number
size=40 value=1 name=retry></TD>
 </TR>

</tbody>
</table>
<br>
<table border="1" cellpadding="0" cellspacing="0"
style="border-collapse: collapse"
bordercolor="#111111" width="100%">
<h4>Payload</h4>
<tbody>
<tr>
<fieldset style="padding: 2">
<td width="50%"><input type="radio" name="Source"
value="Textarea" checked="checked" />Type in XML</td>
<td width="50%"><input type="radio" name="Source"
value="File" />Upload File</td>
</fieldset>
</tr>
<tr>
<td width="50%"><textarea name="xmlData" rows="10"
cols="60">&lt;a&gt;test&lt;/a&gt;</textarea></td>
<td width="50%"><input type="file" name="xmlFile"
size="40" /> </td>
</tr>
</tbody>
</table>
<p>
<input type="button" value="Send" id="button1"
name="button1" LANGUAGE="javascript"
onclick="button1_onclick()" />
</p>
<hr />
<table border="1" cellpadding="0" cellspacing="0"
style="border-collapse: collapse"
bordercolor="#111111" width="100%">
```

```
<h4>Result</h4>
  <P align=left>URL: <TEXTAREA name=URL
cols=104></TEXTAREA></P>
  <P align=left> </P>
<tbody>
<tr>
<td width="50%"><textarea name="response" rows="5"
cols="60"></textarea></td>
</tr>
</tbody>
</table>
</form>

</body>

</html>
```

The code is now updated to allow multiple messages and for new input fields for User and Password.

This HTML code was originally introduced by Joachim Orb for educational purposes.

Question 36: File adapter Wildcard

Is it possible to read files with different names with one (1) file adapter communication channel?

Ex: I want to read all the files that start with "abc".

A: Yes, it is possible.

This is an example of how you do it.

abc*

Take note that it is case sensitive.

Question 37: Sync Receiver JDBC Adapter

I tried to make a synchronous call to a receiver JDBC adapter with the help of a certain helpful website.

I got the following error in the JDBC adapter:

```
com.sap.aii.af.ra.ms.api.DeliveryException:
ERROR:Processing request: Error when executing
statement for table/stored proc. 'MISDetails':
java.sql.SQLException: FATAL ERROR document format:
structure 'STATEMENT', key element 'FiscalYear'
contains no values
```

My Source message is:

```
<?xml version="1.0" encoding="UTF-8"?>
<ns:MT_FILE_OUT xmlns:ns="urn:ters">
<REQUEST>
<FISCALYEAR>2007</FISCALYEAR>
<YEARMONTH>1</YEARMONTH>
<OPERATION>EQ</OPERATION>
</REQUEST>
</ns:MT_FILE_OUT>
And JDBC request message is ..
<?xml version="1.0" encoding="UTF-8"?>
<ns:MT_JDBC_REQ xmlns:ns="urn:ters">
<STATEMENT>
<TABLENAMEACTION="SELECT">
<TABLE>MISDetails</TABLE>
</TABLENAME>
<ACCESS>
<FiscalYear> </FiscalYear>
<YearMonth> </YearMonth><ProductCode>
</ProductCode><TargetVolume> </TargetVolume>
</ACCESS>
<KEY>
<FiscalYear compareOperation="EQ">2007</FiscalYear>
</KEY>
</STATEMENT>
</ns:MT_JDBC_REQ>
```

Can you help me sort this out?

A: The problem is that </TABLENAME> was closed earlier than necessary.

This is how the JDBC data type should be:

```
<?xml version="1.0" encoding="UTF-8"?>
<ns:MT_JDBC_REQ xmlns:ns="urn:ters">
<STATEMENT>
<TABLENAME ACTION="SELECT">
<TABLE>MISDetails</TABLE>
<ACCESS>
<FiscalYear> </FiscalYear>
<YearMonth> </YearMonth>
<ProductCode> </ProductCode>
<TargetVolume> </TargetVolume>
</ACCESS>
<KEY>
<FiscalYear compareOperation="EQ">2007</FiscalYear>
</KEY>
</TABLENAME>
</STATEMENT>
</ns:MT_JDBC_REQ>
```

The TABLE, ACCESS and KEY come under the TABLENAME tag.

Question 38: Outbound File Adapter

I am trying to create an outbound file adapter, designed to receive XML messages from XI Integration engine and store it in a file.

Reading from the document "Configuring the Receiver File/FTP Adapter",

http://help.sap.com/saphelp_nw04/helpdata/en/bc/bb79d6061 007419a081e58cbeaaf28/content.htm

I believe that configuration should look like this:

```
----------------------------------------
## file adapter java class
classname=com.sap.aii.messaging.adapter.ModuleXMB2FIL
E
version=30

mode=XMB2FILE

##Bind the address for Integration port to connect to
XI.httpPort=1981
XI.httpService=/TempFileTran

file.TargetFilename=mindichFile.txt
file.writeMode=overwrite
----------------------------------------
```

The response I receive is "version not set" and adapter docs not start running.

Is there a way to correct this? I use a XI 2.0 SR1.

A: The configuration "version=30" has to be removed. It is not needed in the file adapter.

Although the documentation specifically mentions the fact that "version=30" must exists, it is version dependent.

If you use J2SE adapters to connect with XI3, you may need to put the version configuration.

Question 39: J2SE Adapter Registration

I attempted to use SLD Access service on J2SE adapter, but it does not work. This J2SE Adapter Engine is registered in the SLD. My J2SE adapter was never available in the configuration means; in the communication channel ex: file adapter, the adapter engine drop down and all I have is Integration Server. My J2SE adapter was never listed there.

How do you register J2SE adapter with XI?

A: First, see page 10 of "SAP XI Release 3.0 SR1" installation guide.

http://help.sap.com/bp_bpmv130/Documentation/Installation/ XI30InstallGuide.pdf#search=%22SAP%20XI%20SR1%20instal lation%20guide%22

It mentions the disadvantage of just plain J2SE adapter engine as "Less integration into the SAP XI environment due to lack of central configuration and monitoring services".

It makes sense because in SLD you can only create technical/business system as Web AS Java (say for J2EE decentralized adapter engine) and not as J2SE adapter engine.

But if you want a receiver file adapter, you need to maintain in the adapter configuration:

```
XI.httpPort=<port_no>
XI.httpService=<service>
```

Then in the communication channel, you choose XI protocol (XI 3.0) and as URL you enter:

http://<J2SE-host>:<port_no>/<service>

eg:

```
XI.httpPort=1234
XI.httpService=/file/Receiver
```

-> http://<J2SE-host>:1234/file/Receiver

The file adapter business system needs to be created in SLD to which you will send the message using XML protocol (XI Adapter). The standalone adapter in the business system will then do the XMB2File conversion.

Question 40: Problem with SOAP adapter

I have configured the SOAP adapter to send a message through to a WS-I compliant web service.

I received the following error message:

```
<?xml version="1.0" encoding="UTF-8" standalone="yes"
?>
- <!-- Call Adapter
-->
- <SAP:Error
xmlns:SAP="http://sap.com/xi/XI/Message/30"
xmlns:SOAP="http://schemas.xmlsoap.org/soap/envelope/
" SOAP:mustUnderstand="1">
<SAP:Category>XIAdapter</SAP:Category>
<SAP:Code
area="PARSING">ADAPTER.SOAP_EXCEPTION</SAP:Code>
<SAP:P1 />
<SAP:P2 />
<SAP:P3 />
<SAP:P4 />
<SAP:AdditionalText>soap fault: Server did not
recognize the value of HTTP Header SOAPAction:
.</SAP:AdditionalText>
<SAP:ApplicationFaultMessage namespace="" />
<SAP:Stack />
<SAP:Retry>M</SAP:Retry>
</SAP:Error>
```

Can you point me to the right direction?

A: Your server requires a SOAP-Action.

If you have a WSDL for the message, look at the attributesoapAction of the tag soap:operation. Take the parameter there and type the value in the SOAP adapter receiver channel configuration.

Question 41: RFC Adapter as Sender

We have a business scenario wherein I have to execute the RFC function (asynchronous) from an ABAP in R/3 and update the data in DB2 tables (asynchronous).

I used RFC as sender (asynchronous) and JDBC as receiver (asynchronous). I configured/registered the RFC connection in SM59 and used the same program id in RFC sender adapter. I tested the connection in standalone mode and it is working.

The RFC function, when I imported, will have a request and a response. The data that I require to send to JDBC adapter is in the response. I tried to use RFC response and created a message interface. Then I used that in my interface mapping and also in the sender & receiver agreements. In the message mapping I used, a response was imported.

I got an error message "sender agreement not found". I changed the sender agreement to use RFC function as sender interface, but I cannot use this function module for my mapping, as it does not contain the response.

I deleted the sender/receiver agreements and receiver/interface determination. Then I started creating a new interface determination, but I can't find the interface mapping as the interface mapping user response.

In my business scenario I need a user interface before calling the RFC function. I wrote a wrapper around the RFC that will provide me with user interface; then I would like to send the response data to XI using RFC sender.

We are on XI3.0 SP13. I have to use the response of the RFC in the message mapping. It should be able to send the data to JDBC Adapter.

How do I fix this?

A: If you want to capture the response of an RFC execution in XI and then map this response to another structure (in your case a JDBC structure) inside XI message mapping, then you will have to use the RFC receiver adapter of XI and NOT the RFC sender adapter. If you use the RFC sender adapter, it means that your SAP system is acting as an RFC CLIENT. What happens is the REQUEST structure in your RFC destination will be converted to RFC-XML by the RFC sender adapter of XI and is available for further processing.

If you want to send the RESPONSE structure of an RFC to XI , one way is to execute the RFC in SAP (without passing this thru XI). Now you have to pass the result of this RFC execution to XI by assigning it to a request structure of another RFC in your ABAP code and pass it to XI using RFC sender adapter. If not , you can use a dummy RFC in SAP to send a trigger to XI, execute the actual RFC in XI using RFC receiver adapter, capture the response, map it to your JDBC structure and you are done.

Question 42: JDBC Adapter

I have a scenario where I have to take data from a Relational Database System, the sender, and invoke a BAPI in the receiver system.

How do I get the JDBC adapter to read only entries in DB that has been newly created and not the ones that has been read earlier?

A: You need to have some sort of flag set in the DB table so that every time the Sender Adapter reads the data, it updates the flag accordingly. Do the following:

- Set the polling interval set in the sender JDBC adapter.
- Write your query in the Sender JDBC adapter.

Refer to this thread "JDBC Sender Update Query".

Question 43: IDoc and HTTP Adapters - Sender Agreement

I understand that we don't need to use sender agreement for IDoc and HTTP adapters, because they are sitting right on the ABAP stack. But we do use receiver adapter and receiver agreements even though these two adapters are on ABAP stack.

Can you give an explanation or a link that can explain this clearly?

A: Sender agreement for IDoc and HTTP adapters can be created when necessary. This is if we want to use Adapter-Specific Message Attributes for the http adapter, for example.

The following link explains why we use sender agreements (security, adapter attributes, etc.) Specifically, check the section on Obligatory Sender Agreements.

http://help.sap.com/saphelp_nw04/helpdata/en/b1/f29e7a56e18a439984a3c6630951d2/content.htm

This links tells where exactly Idoc adapter comes into picture; also architecture.

http://help.sap.com/saphelp_nw04/helpdata/en/ab/bdb13b00ae793be10000000a11402f/content.htm

And this, for HTTP (read last 2 paragraphs of the section on Integration).

http://help.sap.com/saphelp_nw04/helpdata/en/44/79973cc73af456e10000000a114084/content.htm

Question 44: Receiver JDBC Adapter

My scenario is an R/3 to XI to JDBC. When any error is encountered in the receiver end, will the JDBC adapter retry?

There is no error on the XI part. In RWB to Communication channel monitoring, I got the error (I simulated the error by giving wrong database/table name).

The msg in Commn. channel monitoring is:

Error while parsing or executing XML-SQL document: Error processing request in sax parser: Error when executing statement for table/stored proc. 'Employee'(structure 'STATEMENTNAME'): java.sql.SQLException: [SQL0204] Employee in SARJAI type *FILE not found.
8/30/06 1:15:36 PM 44f4a7b2b2c417ce01000000ac130c39

Processing started.

I expected to get the message only once, but I got it four times. The interface got triggered only once and there is only 1 message in SXMB_MONI.

I didn't know why it happened? Can you please explain?

A: The most probable reason for the error occurring four times is that the IS_Retry parameter was set to 4 times.

The parameter QRFC_RESTART_ALLOWED is used to restart the queues if it is stuck for whatever reasons.

All messages will go thru this message queues in XI. Once adapter puts messages in the integration engine, it will be in message queues. It is administrated in the transaction code SXMB_ADM->Manage Queues.

Question 45: AE_DETAILS_ GET_ERROR

I tried to configure an HTTP to XI to mail scenario. I received the following error in SXMB_MONI:

```
<?xml version="1.0" encoding="UTF-8" standalone="yes"
?>
- <!-- Call Adapter
-->
- <SAP:Error
xmlns:SAP="http://sap.com/xi/XI/Message/30"
xmlns:SOAP="http://schemas.xmlsoap.org/soap/envelope/
" SOAP:mustUnderstand="1">
<SAP:Category>XIServer</SAP:Category>
<SAP:Code
area="INTERNAL">AE_DETAILS_GET_ERROR</SAP:Code>
<SAP:P1>af.xid.sap1</SAP:P1>
<SAP:P2 />
<SAP:P3 />
<SAP:P4 />
<SAP:AdditionalText>3: Unable to find URL for Adapter
Engine af.xid.sap1</SAP:AdditionalText>
<SAP:ApplicationFaultMessage namespace="" />
<SAP:Stack>Error when reading the access data (URL,
user, password) for the Adapter Engine
af.xid.sap1</SAP:Stack>
<SAP:Retry>M</SAP:Retry>
</SAP:Error>
```

I am not sure, whether this is related to sender HTTP or receiver Mail adapter.

Can you give any solution to this?

A: Some websites can be accessed only if you disable your firewall or configure it correctly to handle the transactions with the said websites.

Normally, this error occurs because of your adapter engine has a case sensitive issue.

MAPPING

Question 46: Multi mapping

Will multi mapping always produce 2 or more target messages?

Based on some source message, I need to decide the target mapping, say field "Receiver" in source. If the value is "1", I need to map the source with target1 message and if the value is 2 I need to map the source with target2 message. Is this possible?

A: The scenario you mentioned can be done using multi mapping. Multi mapping is when multiple messages are involved in the mapping in either the source or the target.

Check for the condition and then create the target mapping. You will need to check for the condition for every field of the target during mapping though.

As your target field creation depends on some condition, you will have to make the check against the source field for every target field.

Question 47: Graphical Mapping

I created a mapping between my file structures to the BAPI structure. This is actually the file that will call BAPI for 1: N (file having various headers and line items, each header and associated line items will be able to call BAPI in target side).

I tested the said mapping, but the following error came when I checked in the Interface Mapping.

ERROR: Mapping program Message Mapping MM_request | urn:testing does not match the interface mapping. The number or frequencies of source or target messages for the message mapping are not identical to the number or frequencies of source or target interfaces.

But when I did the test in the MM editor using duplicate subtree, it works fine.

I did the mapping like this:

```
Sourcefilestructure: TargetBAPI
------------------------------------------------
Messages (1:1) Message(1:1)
Message1(1:1) Message1(1:1)
MT_Request(1:1)
Recordset(0:U)  --> BAPI_INCOMINGINVOICE(0:U)
HDR (0:1) HeaderData(1:1)
Filed(0:1) --> filed1(0:1)
Field(0:1) --> field2(0:2)
HDR---> GLACCOUNTDATA(0:1)
LINEITEM(0:U)---> item(0:U)
field1(0:1) ---> field(0:1)
field2(0:1) ---> field2(0:1)
```

Can you give me any idea where I made the error?

A: You are doing your multi mapping right and you have changed the occurrences in the message tab in the message mapping.

Check if you changed the occurrences in the interface mapping. The reason for this is because in the last column, there is an occurrence.

You will have this kind of error message when inside your Interface Mapping you used occurrences that are NOT the one defined in your Message Mapping.

In your message mapping, look at the tab "Message" and keep in mind the occurrences.

Then in your Interface Mapping, do the same action and compare both occurrences.

Question 48: Unlock a Message Mapping

I work remote via VPN on my XI server. The VPN was suddenly disconnected while I was working on a message mapping. After reconnecting and restarting the repository, I tried to work on the message mapping again, but XI open a dialog with the information that the mapping is already in work by my user.

Where can I unlock this?

A: You will have to go to the XI Home Page, then access 'Administration', then 'Lock Overview', and then unlock your objects.

Question 49: N:1 Mapping Possible using Java Mapping

Is it possible to do an N:1 mapping using Java Mapping? If possible, how?

The reason for this question is that the 'execute()' of the Java Mapping is going to take the source / request message as the Input Stream. In the case of N:1 mapping, as we have multiple messages, how will they be sent to the Input Stream? Will both the messages be sent combined into the Input Stream? Will the MESSAGE tag be embedded into the input stream?

A: Yes, it is possible to do an N: 1 mapping using Java Mapping.

For multiple messages, XI's input stream will be something like:

```
<ns0:Messages
xmlns:ns0="http://sap.com/xi/XI/SplitAndMerge">
<ns0:Message1>
<YOURXML1>...</YOURXML1>
</ns0:Message1>
<ns0:Message2>
<YOURXML2>...</YOURXML2>
</ns0:Message2>
<ns0:Messages>
```

So, your root tag will be messages and inside each "messageX" you will find your input messages exactly like the source code for the source messages in Interface Mapping test tab.

This approach works for both Java and XSLT multi mappings.

Question 50: Mapping Test

What is the difference between "Test Tab under Message Mapping" and "Test Tab under Interface Mapping"?

A: "Test Tab under message mapping" can only be used to test graphical mapping. It is a test at message level.

"Test tab under interface mapping" can test XSLT / Graphical / Java. This test is at interface level.

For more details concerning this discussion, visit the following links.

Message Mapping Test

http://help.sap.com/saphelp_nw04/helpdata/en/c3/e3072e65f 04445a010847aa970b68b/content.htm

Interface Mapping Test

http://help.sap.com/saphelp_nw04/helpdata/en/db/86of1ee5f 945d699a717cd9b4512a7/content.htm

Question 51: "No steps" Mapping & Determination in Pipeline (SXMB_MONI)

I'm using a SAP/R3 IDoc->XI->IDoc SAP/R3 with IDoc RSINFO. All is fine and works well.

But in SXMB_MONI, I don't see pipeline steps:

- Receiver determination
- Interface determination

I only see:

- Inbound message (central)
- Receiver grouping
- Response

Is there any way of customizing to log and see those steps?

A: To specifically see all the logging desired in SXMB_MONI, use SXMB_ADM and set the following flags to "1";

category/parameter
RUNTIME/LOGGING
RUNTIME/LOGGING_PROPAGATION
RUNTIME/LOGGING_SYNC

These logging parameters should be set only on DEV systems, as they will introduce additional disk space requirement.

Question 52: *Mapping Flat Structure in Complex Structure*

Is it possible to use graphical mapping to obtain the following result?

I have this example input message type:

```xml
<?xml version="1.0" encoding="UTF-8"?>
<ns0:MT_CONFERMA xmlns:ns0="http://prova">
<HEADER>
<TRASM>1</TRASM>
<MDI>1234</MDI>
</HEADER>
<HEADER>
<TRASM>2</TRASM>
<MDI>2657</MDI>
</HEADER>
<ROW>
<TRASM>1</TRASM>
<RNUM>1.1</RNUM>
<ART>1.1</ART>
</ROW>
<ROW>
<TRASM>1</TRASM>
<RNUM>1.2</RNUM>
<ART>1.2</ART>
</ROW>
<ROW>
<TRASM>2</TRASM>
<RNUM>2.1</RNUM>
<ART>2.1</ART>
</ROW>
<ROW>
<TRASM>2</TRASM>
<RNUM>2.2</RNUM>
<ART>2.2</ART>
</ROW>
</ns0:MT_CONFERMA>
```

Result:

```
<ns0:MT_OUT xmlns:ns0="http://prova">
<DATA>
<TRASM>1</TRASM>
<MDI>1234</MDI>
<ROW>
<TRASM>1</TRASM>
<RNUM>1.1</RNUM>
<ART>1.1</ART>
</ROW>
<ROW>
<TRASM>1</TRASM>
<RNUM>1.2</RNUM>
<ART>1.2</ART>
</ROW>
</DATA>
<DATA>
<TRASM>2</TRASM>
<MDI>2657</MDI>
<ROW>
<TRASM>2</TRASM>
<RNUM>2.1</RNUM>
<ART>2.1</ART>
</ROW>
<ROW>
<TRASM>2</TRASM>
<RNUM>2.2</RNUM>
<ART>2.2</ART>
</ROW>
</DATA>
</ns0:MT_OUT>
```

The split data is "TRASM". I tried some methods but without the correct solution.

Can you help me solve this?

A: Yes. Apply this correction:

```
CONFERMA - > MT_OUT
HEADER -> DATA
TRASM - >TRASM
MDI - >MDI

ROW:

TRASM (cont. CONFERMA)- >split(byvalue-value
change)ROW
RNUM- >RNUM
ART->ART
```

Question 53: XI XML to IDoc Mapping

I have a scenario where I have an XML to IDoc mapping. I have
an XML sent from an SCM system and IDoc is getting converted
in the XI, but the IDoc that is getting created in the R/3 does not
have the data that is contained in the XML. The control
structure in the IDoc does not have the message variant
populated in the IDoc, whereas in the SXMB_MONI, I could see
the IDoc (XML format) containing this data.

The system has the note 886263 implemented. Can I check the
XML within the R/3 system?

A: You will need to check these things first.

1.   Is the control record fields filled up or not in the R/3
      system?
2.   Do you want to manipulate the Control Record from XI?
      Have you selected the option, Apply Control Record from
      payload, take sender from payload, take receiver from
      payload in the IDoc adapter?

Your control structure must have been partially filled with the
message type but the message variant is not filled in the XI.

You may need to enable the check box for the Apply control
record values for the payload for it to work.

Question 54: Defining Content Conversion and Mapping

We have a situation where a flat file looks somewhat like the following:
```
name,age
city,country
id,number
dept,wing
```

Now in the flat file, the input may vary as shown below:
```
name,age
city,country
id,number
dept,wing
name1,age1
city1,country1
id1,number1
dept1,wing1
```

Or:
```
name,age
city,country
id,number
dept,wing
name1,age1
city1,country1
name2,age2
city2,country2
```

Or:
```
id,number
dept,wing
id1,number1
dept1,wing1
name,age
city,country
```

Or:
```
name,age
city,country
name1,age1
city1,country1
```

Or:
```
id,number
dept,wing
id1,number1
dept1,wing1
```

In short, the <name,age> will always be followed by <city,country> and <id,number> by <dept,wing> but the combinations occur in random, for example, <name,age> & <city,country> may come before the <id,number> & <dept,wing> or vice versa.

We do make use of key fields. But when the combinations occur in random, how do we define its content conversion and mapping?

A: The answer lies in defining the source data type. It may look something like this:

```
Dt_input
|
Details (0-Unbounded)
|_title (0-Unbounded)
|_name
|_age
|_info(0-Unbounded)
|_city
|_country
|_tag(0-Unbounded)
|_id
|_number
|_node(0-Unbounded)
|_dept
|_wing
```

During content conversion, treat the recordset as details and the recordset structure as title,*,info,*,tag,*,node,*;. You can also specify the recordset per message as *.

Question 55: Mapping Problem

I was working on a scenario file to R/3. I received the following error message in SXMB_MONI:

"mapping exception during execute"

I checked the mapping in IR to Mapping test. The result message is:

```
Messages:
13:16:40 Start of test
Unparseable date: "06.04."
com.sap.aii.utilxi.misc.api.BaseRuntimeException:
Unparseable date:
"06.04."
at
com.sap.aii.mappingtool.flib3.DateTransformer.convert
Date(DateTransformer.ja
va:39)
at
com.sap.aii.mappingtool.flib3.DateTransformer.getValu
e(DateTransformer.java:
27)
at
com.sap.aii.mappingtool.tf3.AMappingProgram.processNo
de(AMappingProgram.java
:369)
at
com.sap.aii.mappingtool.tf3.AMappingProgram.processNo
de(AMappingProgram.java
:387)
at
com.sap.aii.mappingtool.tf3.AMappingProgram.processNo
de(AMappingProgram.java
:387)
at
com.sap.aii.mappingtool.tf3.AMappingProgram.processNo
de(AMappingProgram.java
:387)
at
com.sap.aii.mappingtool.tf3.AMappingProgram.start(AMa
ppingProgram.java:287)
at
com.sap.aii.mappingtool.tf3.Transformer.start(Transfo
rmer.java:63)
at
```

```
com.sap.aii.mappingtool.tf3.AMappingProgram.execute(A
MappingProgram.java:232
)
at
com.sap.aii.ibrep.server.mapping.ServerMapService.tra
nsformInternal(ServerMa
pService.java:432)
at
com.sap.aii.ibrep.server.mapping.ServerMapService.exe
cute(ServerMapService.j
ava:170)
at
com.sap.aii.ibrep.sbeans.mapping.MapServiceBean.execu
te(MapServiceBean.java:
52)
at
com.sap.aii.ibrep.sbeans.mapping.MapServiceRemoteObje
ctImpl0.execute(MapServ
iceRemoteObjectImpl0.java:259)
at
com.sap.aii.ibrep.sbeans.mapping.MapServiceRemoteObje
ctImpl0p4_Skel.dispatch
(MapServiceRemoteObjectImpl0p4_Skel.java:146)
at
com.sap.engine.services.rmi_p4.DispatchImpl._runInter
nal(DispatchImpl.java:2
94)
at
com.sap.engine.services.rmi_p4.DispatchImpl._run(Disp
atchImpl.java:183)
at
com.sap.engine.services.rmi_p4.server.P4SessionProces
sor.request(P4SessionPr
ocessor.java:119)
at
com.sap.engine.core.service630.context.cluster.sessio
n.ApplicationSessionMes
sageListener.process(ApplicationSessionMessageListene
r.java:37)
at
com.sap.engine.core.cluster.impl6.session.UnorderedCh
annel$MessageRunner.run
(UnorderedChannel.java:71)
at
com.sap.engine.core.thread.impl3.ActionObject.run(Act
ionObject.java:37)
at java.security.AccessController.doPrivileged(Native
Method)
at
```

```
com.sap.engine.core.thread.impl3.SingleThread.execute
(SingleThread.java:95)
at
com.sap.engine.core.thread.impl3.SingleThread.run(Sin
gleThread.java:159)
Root Cause:
java.text.ParseException: Unparseable date: "06.04."
at java.text.DateFormat.parse(DateFormat.java:335)
at
com.sap.aii.mappingtool.flib3.DateTransformer.convert
Date(DateTransformer.ja
va:35)
at
com.sap.aii.mappingtool.flib3.DateTransformer.getValu
e(DateTransformer.java:
27)
at
com.sap.aii.mappingtool.tf3.AMappingProgram.processNo
de(AMappingProgram.java
:369)
at
com.sap.aii.mappingtool.tf3.AMappingProgram.processNo
de(AMappingProgram.java
:387)
at
com.sap.aii.mappingtool.tf3.AMappingProgram.processNo
de(AMappingProgram.java
:387)
at
com.sap.aii.mappingtool.tf3.AMappingProgram.processNo
de(AMappingProgram.java
:387)
at
com.sap.aii.mappingtool.tf3.AMappingProgram.start(AMa
ppingProgram.java:287)
at
com.sap.aii.mappingtool.tf3.Transformer.start(Transfo
rmer.java:63)
at
com.sap.aii.mappingtool.tf3.AMappingProgram.execute(A
MappingProgram.java:232
)
at
com.sap.aii.ibrep.server.mapping.ServerMapService.tra
nsformInternal(ServerMa
pService.java:432)
at
com.sap.aii.ibrep.server.mapping.ServerMapService.exe
cute(ServerMapService.j
```

```
ava:170)
at
com.sap.aii.ibrep.sbeans.mapping.MapServiceBean.execu
te(MapServiceBean.java:
52)
at
com.sap.aii.ibrep.sbeans.mapping.MapServiceRemoteObje
ctImpl0.execute(MapServ
iceRemoteObjectImpl0.java:259)
at
com.sap.aii.ibrep.sbeans.mapping.MapServiceRemoteObje
ctImpl0p4_Skel.dispatch
(MapServiceRemoteObjectImpl0p4_Skel.java:146)
at
com.sap.engine.services.rmi_p4.DispatchImpl._runInter
nal(DispatchImpl.java:2
94)
at
com.sap.engine.services.rmi_p4.DispatchImpl._run(Disp
atchImpl.java:183)
at
com.sap.engine.services.rmi_p4.server.P4SessionProces
sor.request(P4SessionPr
ocessor.java:119)
at
com.sap.engine.core.service630.context.cluster.sessio
n.ApplicationSessionMes
sageListener.process(ApplicationSessionMessageListene
r.java:37)
at
com.sap.engine.core.cluster.impl6.session.UnorderedCh
annel$MessageRunner.run
(UnorderedChannel.java:71)
at
com.sap.engine.core.thread.impl3.ActionObject.run(Act
ionObject.java:37)
at java.security.AccessController.doPrivileged(Native
Method)
at
com.sap.engine.core.thread.impl3.SingleThread.execute
(SingleThread.java:95)
at
com.sap.engine.core.thread.impl3.SingleThread.run(Sin
gleThread.java:159)
13:16:40 End of test
```

Can you give me some pointers in fixing this?

A: There is a date value that your codes were not able to parse. Check if you are using any user defined functions.

```
Unparseable date:
"06.04."
```

This is due to some date transformation problem. Use the correct format;

dd.mm.yyyy or mm.dd.yyyy

For better debugging, you can check the Display Queue option in the Message Mapping in the IR. Check each input values.

You will need to check the input XML. Is it a valid XML? You can check this by saving into notepad with .xml and open in the browser. You can also use XML editors.

Question 56: Mapping Specific Elements to Generic Elements

I need to map source specific elements into target generic elements that are specialized with a "name" attribute. I don't know how I can specify at the same time the "name" attribute's value ("currency" or "edi_currency" for example) depending on the present source elements (CURCY, HWAER, and KUNDEUINR) and copy this source element's value as the target element's value.

This is an example:

Source:

```
<ORDERS05>
<IDOC>
<E1EDK01>
<CURCY>XXX</CURCY>
<HWAER>YYY</HWAER>
<KUNDEUINR>ZZZ</KUNDEUINR>
...
</E1EDK01>
</IDOC>
</ORDERS05>
```

Target:

```
<MYORDER>
<HEADER>
<PROP name="currency">XXX</PROP>
<PROP name="edi_currency">YYY</PROP>
<PROP name="vat_reg_nbr">ZZZ</PROP>
...
</HEADER>
</MYORDER>
```

Can this be done? If so, how?

A: You can do your mapping with standard graphical mapping features. There is no need for a user defined function. A simple "How to" will suffice:

1. Do this mapping:

    CURCY --> PROP
    Constant[currency] -->@name

2. Duplicate the structure PROP. Right click mouse and pick duplicate subtree and map the second occurrence of PROP as follows:

    HWAER --> PROP
    Constant[edi_currency] --> @name

3. Duplicate the structure PROP again and map the third occurrence as follows:

    KUNDEUINR --> PROP
    Constant[vat_reg_nbr] --> @name

Question 57: Java Mapping Error

We have saved java maps in zip files. We are getting the following error when we tried to test it.

```
14:29:25 Start of test
LinkageError at JavaMapping.load(): Could not load
class: build/classes/com/bmwmc/pcard/mapping/Response

java.lang.NoClassDefFoundError:
build/classes/com/bmwmc/pcard/mapping/Response (wrong
name: com/bmwmc/pcard/mapping/Response)
at java.lang.ClassLoader.defineClass0(Native Method)
at
java.lang.ClassLoader.defineClass(ClassLoader.java:53
9)
at
java.lang.ClassLoader.defineClass(ClassLoader.java:44
8)
at
com.sap.aii.ibrep.server.mapping.ibrun.RepMappingLoad
er.findClass(RepMappingLoader.java:175)
at
java.lang.ClassLoader.loadClass(ClassLoader.java:289)
at
java.lang.ClassLoader.loadClass(ClassLoader.java:235)
at
com.sap.aii.ibrep.server.mapping.ibrun.RepJavaMapping
.load(RepJavaMapping.java:136)
at
com.sap.aii.ibrep.server.mapping.ibrun.RepJavaMapping
.execute(RepJavaMapping.java:50)
at
com.sap.aii.ibrep.server.mapping.ibrun.RepMappingHand
ler.run(RepMappingHandler.java:75)
at
com.sap.aii.ibrep.server.mapping.rt.MappingHandlerAda
pter.run(MappingHandlerAdapter.java:107)
at
com.sap.aii.ibrep.server.mapping.ServerMapService.tra
nsformInterfaceMapping(ServerMapService.java:127)
at
com.sap.aii.ibrep.server.mapping.ServerMapService.tra
nsform(ServerMapService.java:104)
at
com.sap.aii.ibrep.sbeans.mapping.MapServiceBean.trans
form(MapServiceBean.java:40)
```

```
at
com.sap.aii.ibrep.sbeans.mapping.MapServiceRemoteObje
ctImpl0.transform(MapServiceRemoteObjectImpl0.java:13
1)
at
com.sap.aii.ibrep.sbeans.mapping.MapServiceRemoteObje
ctImpl0p4_Skel.dispatch(MapServiceRemoteObjectImpl0p4
_Skel.java:104)
at
com.sap.engine.services.rmi_p4.DispatchImpl._runInter
nal(DispatchImpl.java:294)
at
com.sap.engine.services.rmi_p4.DispatchImpl._run(Disp
atchImpl.java:183)
at
com.sap.engine.services.rmi_p4.server.P4SessionProces
sor.request(P4SessionProcessor.java:119)
at
com.sap.engine.core.service630.context.cluster.sessio
n.ApplicationSessionMessageListener.process(Applicati
onSessionMessageListener.java:33)
at
com.sap.engine.core.cluster.impl6.session.MessageRunn
er.run(MessageRunner.java:41)
at
com.sap.engine.core.thread.impl3.ActionObject.run(Act
ionObject.java:37)
at java.security.AccessController.doPrivileged(Native
Method)
at
com.sap.engine.core.thread.impl3.SingleThread.execute
(SingleThread.java:95)
at
com.sap.engine.core.thread.impl3.SingleThread.run(Sin
gleThread.java:159)

14:29:25 End of test
```

Is there any way I can fix this?

A: You need to set the directory structure starting with com in your zip file and not with build/classes for the class files. So your zip has com/bmwmc/pcard/mapping/Response.class instead of build/classes/com/bmwmc/pcard/mapping/Response.

Question 58: RFC to Webservice Interface in XI

I am calling a web service hosted in the Internet from RFC (in SAP R/3) via XI. I have completed the design and configuration activities. But, while I execute the RFC I am getting a short dump with the message:

```
"call to messaging system failed:
com.sap.aii.af.ra.ms.api.DeliveryException:".
```

I had created a sender Communication Channel (type RFC) giving a Program ID. Same Program ID is used in the TCP/IP RFC Destination in R/3. I checked the RFC destination and it is working fine. SAP XI engine is also activated.

I am using two synchronous message interfaces. The outbound interface is RFC and the inbound interface is webservice. I am also getting two messages with Red flag in SXMB_MONI. I checked the run-time workbench and received the following error message:

```
Received XI System Error. ErrorCode:
EXCEPTION_DURING_EXECUTE ErrorText: ErrorStack:
During the application mapping
com/sap/xi/tf/_MM_Webservice_OutputMap_ a
com.sap.aii.utilxi.misc.api.BaseRuntimeExceptio
n was thrown: Fatal Error:
com.sap.engine.lib.xml.parser.Parser~
2006-07-28 11:30:54 Error Returning synchronous
error notification to calling application:
Application:EXCEPTION_DURING_EXECUTE:.
2006-07-28 11:30:54 Error Transmitting the
message using connection
http://ntbomsap11:8000/sap/xi/engine?type=entry
failed, due to:
Application:EXCEPTION_DURING_EXECUTE:.
2006-07-28 11:30:54 Error The message status
set to FAIL.
```

Can you please tell me why this is happening?

A: There are some problems in your message mapping. First, check if your Webservice_OutputMap has the correct structure. Simple guides to check can be found online.

Question 59: ERROR: EXCEPTION_DURING_EXECUTE while using FILE CONTENT CONVERSION

I set up a file-to-file scenario with File Content Conversion for Sender communication channel, but I got the following error in SXMB_MONI:

```
<SAP:Category>Application</SAP:Category>
<SAP:Code
area="MAPPING">EXCEPTION_DURING_EXECUTE</SAP:Code>
<SAP:P1>com/sap/xi/tf/_MM_ContentBased_</SAP:P1>
<SAP:P2>com.sap.aii.utilxi.misc.api.BaseRuntimeExcept
ion</SAP:P2>
<SAP:P3>RuntimeException in Message-Mapping
transformatio~</SAP:P3>
<SAP:P4 />
<SAP:AdditionalText />
<SAP:ApplicationFaultMessage namespace="" />
<SAP:Stack>During the application mapping
com/sap/xi/tf/_MM_ContentBased_ a
com.sap.aii.utilxi.misc.api.BaseRuntimeException was
thrown: RuntimeException in Message-Mapping
transformatio~</SAP:Stack>
<SAP:Retry>M</SAP:Retry>
</SAP:Error>
```

I tried the same message mapping for normal file-to-file scenario without using File Content Conversion. It went through fine.

Our file structure follows:

```
<Header>
<Sysnum>01</Sysnum>
</Header>
<Body>
<Name>ABCDE</Name>
<Age>25</Age>
<Stream>XYZ</Stream>
</Body>
```

The Sender Communication Channel Parameters follows:

```
Recordset Str: Header,1,Body,1
```

```
Header.fieldFixedLengths : 2

Header.fieldNames : Sysnum

Body.fieldFixedLengths : 5,2,3

Body.fieldNames : Name,Age,Stream

ignoreRecordsetName : true
```

How do I make this work?

A: Your message mapping failed. To rectify this, copy the XML message from monitoring and execute the mapping in Integration Builder with maximal trace to get the reason for the failure. From there, it would be easier to plot out corrections.

SENDER & RECEIVER ISSUES

Question 60: RFC Sender Problem (Asynchronous)

Is there a way to detect from a RFC FM asynchronous call if XI is down?

I understand that if the RFC call is asynchronous, no exceptions are caught. But is there a workaround on catching the error?

A: You can use transaction SM58 to restart LUW on your source system. In this transaction you will see all errors in asynchronous RFC communication.

Question 61: Error when Sending Null Records in BPM

In my scenario, I have four (4) Business systems involved.

1. File (Sender)
2. An Oracle DB (Receiver)
3. R3 (Receiver)
4. File (Receiver)

I used a File to R3 (using RFC) Scenario where I have a BPM. In XI, I did some validations and if any of the validations fail, I have to send those error records to a database table (System B). If the records pass the validation, it is sent to R3 (System C) and the count of the successfully updated records (in R3) are sent to System D.

In my BPM, I sent all correct records. There are no error records (no data to be passed to DB).

I received the following error message:

```
<?xml version="1.0" encoding="UTF-8" standalone="yes"
?>
- <!-- Receiver Identification
-->
- <SAP:Error
xmlns:SAP="http://sap.com/xi/XI/Message/30"
xmlns:SOAP="http://schemas.xmlsoap.org/soap/envelope/
" SOAP:mustUnderstand="">
<SAP:Category>XIServer</SAP:Category>
<SAP:Code
area="RCVR_DETERMINATION">MESSAGE_INCOMPLETE</SAP:Cod
e>
<SAP:P1>Sender</SAP:P1>
<SAP:P2 />
<SAP:P3 />
<SAP:P4 />
<SAP:AdditionalText />
<SAP:ApplicationFaultMessage namespace="" />
<SAP:Stack>Message is incomplete. No Sender
found</SAP:Stack>
<SAP:Retry>M</SAP:Retry>
</SAP:Error>
```

The scenario works fine when there are records to be sent to DB.

I used multi mapping in my scenario. Steps in my BPM are:

1. Receive step
2. Transformation Step
3. Block (For Each)
4. Inside the block I have a switch step to do the check (validation)
5. In my first branch I appended the correct records to a multi-line container
6. In the other branch I appended the error messages to a multi-line container
7. Outside the block I have a transformation step for bundling the error records and a send step for sending the error records
8. Next I have another transformation step for bundling the correct records and a send step for sending the correct records. This is a synchronous send step for getting response from R3
9. And then, the final send step for sending the count.

Can you tell me if there is any other option available for such a scenario, because I may have null records for errors? Is there any error handling mechanism available that I can use here?

A: You can actually create the message type and check the flag using a fork or a switch. If it is a valid payload, let it go through the same step; otherwise, don't.

An alternate yet a similar scenario:

1. Receive
2. Transformation (receiver MT, audit MT and error MT all done in one MM)
3. Switch (to check valid condition for sending receiver MT, audit MT and error MT)
4. Block inside switch for each condition and send step in the block.

Question 62: Receiver Determination Step in BPM

I have a BPM process similar to 'Multicat BPM Pattern'. I have some questions regarding how the 'Receiver Determination' works:

1. Does it have to have interface determination in the 'Integration Directory'?
2. Does that interface determination (including the mapping) takes place when sending a message to a receiver from that 'Receiver Determination' step, or should I perform a 'Mapping' step explicitly in the process?

Example:

My source message is A. My receiver requires the message B.

If I define a 'Receiver Determination', and a corresponding 'Interface Determination', which maps the source message A to the message B, and then I use a send step to a receiver from that 'Receiver Determination', do I need to send the message A or the message B?

A:

1. In every 'Receiver Determination', you need to have an 'Interface Determination'.

   Example is given here:

   http://help.sap.com/saphelp_nw2004s/helpdata/en/14/d5283fd0ca8443e10000000a114084/content.htm

2. Receiver From: Receivers List

   It just sends message (A) to the receiver, or also performs the mapping.

If you have given / selected the appropriate 'INTERFACE MAPPING' for 'Interface Determination', then mapping will be performed.

If you have not selected Interface Mapping, then the mapping will not be performed.

Question 63: RFC Receiver

We have a RFC receiver adapter pointing to a client. We want it to point to another R/3 client.

Is it enough to change the adapter specific information regarding the receiver?

A: Yes, the adapter specific information is enough to change the receiver settings.

For more information, visit the following links:

http://help.sap.com/saphelp_nw04/helpdata/en/33/c6e63b60c 25767e10000000a11402f/content.htm

http://help.sap.com/saphelp_nw04/helpdata/en/c8/e80440a8 32e369e10000000a155106/content.htm

Question 64: JDBC Receiver Document Format

I have to pull the data from DB. The SQL Query is:

```
Select field1
from systemName.table
where field2 = field1
order by field1.
```

Can you help me find a way to define the data type to realize the SQL query on the receiver side?

A: You will need to import this ".xsd" as external definition and then proceed.

```
<xsd:schema elementFormDefault="qualified"
xmlns:xsd="http://www.w3.org/2001/XMLSchema">
<xsd:element name="Receiver_JDBC" type="Statement1"/>
<xsd:complexType name="Statement1">
<xsd:sequence>
<xsd:element name="statement1">
<xsd:complexType>
<xsd:sequence>
<xsd:element name="Vishal">
<xsd:complexType>
<xsd:sequence>
<xsd:element name="access"/>
<xsd:element name="key">
<xsd:complexType>
<xsd:sequence></xsd:sequence>
</xsd:complexType>
</xsd:element>
</xsd:sequence>
<xsd:attribute name="action">
<xsd:simpleType>
<xsd:restriction base="xsd:string">
<xsd:pattern value-"SQL_QUERY|SQL_DML"/>
</xsd:restriction>
</xsd:simpleType>
</xsd:attribute>
</xsd:complexType>
</xsd:element>
</xsd:sequence>
</xsd:complexType>
</xsd:element>
```

```
</xsd:sequence>
</xsd:complexType>
</xsd:schema>
```

You can generate this ".xsd" using XML spy or any other XML tool.

You can use "SQL_QUERY" or "SQL_DML", but you lose the dynamic of your request.

I would recommend you to use action "SELECT" like describe in library. The problem is the clause "order by" can't be solved this way in JDBC adapter, but easy with an (additional) XSLT mapping.

Use element xsl:sort as child from xsl:apply-templates or xsl:for-each. Use if necessary, attribute orders with values ascending or descending. Use may be attributed to data-type with values "number"/"text".

Question 65: Unable to Determine Receiver

I encountered a problem in Receiver Determination. The error is generated at the Receiver Grouping tag in SXMB_MONI. The error description is "Unable to Determine receiver (processing type:QOS = EO or EOIO)".

Below is the trace snippet where the error is getting generated.

```
<Trace level="1" type="System_Error">Exit XMB because
of system error!</Trace>
<Trace level="3" type="System_Error">System-Error:
ROUTING.NO_RECEIVER_CASE_ASYNC</Trace>
<Trace level="3" type="System_Error">Unable to
determine a receiver (processing type: QoS = EO or
EOIO)</Trace>
<Trace level="1" type="Timestamp">2004-08-
05T16:36:52ZEnd of pipeline service processing
PLSRVID= PLSRV_RECEIVER_DETERMINATION</Trace>
```

Can you help me correct this problem?

A: You need to check if you have created namespace correctly.

Verify if you have the namespace created with "http://..." and not "http:\\...." Do not use this slash (\) or backslash, as the system considers it as an escape character and therefore it does not work.

Question 66: JDBC Receiver Action Select

I have this problem with a JDBC Receiver Adapter. I want to synchronize a process form a Web service to TeraData Database. The deployed driver works, and I can get Data with JDBC Sender Adapter, but I received this error:

```
<?xml version="1.0" encoding="UTF-8" standalone="yes"
?>
- <!-- Aufruf eines Adapters
-->
- <SAP:Error
xmlns:SAP="http://sap.com/xi/XI/Message/30"
xmlns:SOAP="http://schemas.xmlsoap.org/soap/envelope/
" SOAP:mustUnderstand="1">
<SAP:Category>XIAdapterFramework</SAP:Category>
<SAP:Code area="MESSAGE">GENERAL</SAP:Code>
<SAP:P1 />
<SAP:P2 />
<SAP:P3 />
<SAP:P4 />
<SAP:AdditionalText>com.sap.aii.af.ra.ms.api.Delivery
Exception: Error processing request in sax parser: No
'action' attribute found in XML document (attribute
"action" missing or wrong XML
structure)</SAP:AdditionalText>
<SAP:ApplicationFaultMessage namespace="" />
<SAP:Stack />
<SAP:Retry>M</SAP:Retry>
</SAP:Error>
```

But the structure is the same as on the sap help:

```
<M_VerlagSelect>
<verlag action="SELECT">
<table>verlag</table>
<access>
<Objekt />
<Objekt_Bezeichnung />
<Level />
</access>
<key1>
<Verlag>10000</Verlag>
<Level>0</Level>
</key1>
```

```
</pvg_usrObjekt>
</M_VerlagSelect>
```

JDBC Adapter Receiver

Can you help me fix this?

A: Yes. The problem is you have missed the STATEMENT tag,

```
<M_VerlagSelect>
<STATEMENT>
<verlag action="SELECT">
<table>verlag</table>
<access>
<Objekt />
<Objekt_Bezeichnung />
<Level />
</access>
<key1>
<Verlag>10000</Verlag>
<Level>0</Level>
</key1>
</pvg_usrObjekt>
</STATEMENT>
</M_VerlagSelect>
```

You have a tag </pvg_usrObjekt>. It should be either inside KEY 1 or KEY2 and so on.

Question 67: Configuration Error in Receiving SAP R/3

I configured a File to XI to R/3 (ABAP Proxy) scenario. When I checked in SXMB_MONI, it gave me an error in XI. I received the following error ID in SXMB_MONI:

```
"SYSTEM_NOT_CONFIGURED_AS XMB".
```

Can you help me figure this out?

A: You need to go and check in the Receiving R/3 system.

Access the following:

SXMB_ADM, then Configuration, then Integration Engine Configuration, then choose your R/3 system as Application System.

Question 68: Set Message's Party inside BPM

We have a scenario where a business system sends a message to XI, a BPM receives it, and depending on the value of a field, the BPM should determine the party where to send the message.

I know how to obtain the Sender or Receiver Party in a transformation, but not how to set it.

How can I send the party to a message?

A: BPM does not send the message to the party. You have to define a receiver agreement for you BPM (your BPM is a service in ID).

So when BPM sends the message via a send step, the message goes from the workflow-engine to the integration engine.

There in the integration engine, the ID, and in your receiver determination, you can maintain conditions for the receivers.

Question 69: BPM or not?

I need to pull data from an Oracle database and query SAP table from the data pulled from Oracle. Based on the data from SAP, the data should be updated into the Oracle Database.

This has to happen on a daily basis at 7 am.

Should I go for a BPM or could it be done in an interface?

A: You definitely need to go for BPM. You need to use a sender JDBC adapter to pull in the data into XI.

Here are steps in using BPM:

1. Receive data from Oracle.
2. Send sync data to SAP.
3. Map the response from SAP to the DB for updating (receiver JDBC).

To run a BPM at a certain time, there's a couple of links I advise you to visit.

Question 70: RFC Sends Data to an SQL Server

I'm trying to make a simple scenario where RFC sends data to an SQL server. I made all the mappings interfaces, etc. When I execute make a dump, this error occurs:

"Server repository could not create a function template"

Can you help me correct this?

A: Make sure that you have defined the appropriate server settings for "RFC Metadata Repository" in the RFC Sender Adapter settings. It must point to a server where the function is defined. The sender adapter accesses the RFC metadata at runtime.

GENERAL XI CONFIGURATION

Question 71: Comparing Data from 2 Tables

This is a JDBC-Proxy scenario. I used a JDBC sender adapter to pick records from the table and used a proxy to pass the data to R/3 and called a function module in R/3. The scenario worked fine as expected.

There is another table in the database that contains the history. I need to compare the records in the 2 tables and pass the data to R/3 if a record does not exist in second table. But if a record exists, I need to check for the "amount" field again. If the amount in the history file is lesser, the record has to be passed with the amount (difference between the first table and history table). If the amount is also the same, I should not send the record to R/3.

How can I do these comparisons and then pass the data to R/3?

A: You need a BPM and you need to select the data from the database for the history table. Then do a mapping and determine whether IDoc is to be sent out or not. The steps are as follows:

1. Receive - select data from Table 1
2. Send Sync - select data from table 2
3. Transformation (n:1) - combine the data from step 1 and step 2 and do the mapping. Set a field to determine if the IDoc should be sent or not
4. Switch - check for the data and then send the IDoc if needed, otherwise terminate the BPM and process flow.

Question 72: Server Proxy not executed - Not updating Data

I am currently working on a File to XI to ECC 5.0 scenario. The message reached ECC side and the status in SXMB_MONI is filed and contained the payload. I have tested the proxy interface from SPROXY and it works fine (updating the database).

But in runtime it's not updating the database. It seems that it is not executing the method "EXECUTE_ASYNCHRONOUS". I was not able to see it in SM51 though it has an infinite loop.

Can you give some advice concerning this?

A: You need to go and check the error that shows in the SXMB_MONI of your ECC system. Make sure that queues are registered correctly in the ECC system. To do this, you need to access 'SXMB_ADM', then 'Manage Queues', then 'Register All'.

Question 73: File to XI to JDBC Error

I was processing a file to JDBC scenario that I took as an example from this link:

https://www.sdn.sap.com/irj/sdn/weblogs?blog=/pub/wlg/1772

I received the following error in the JDBC adapter monitoring:

```
Receiver Adapter v2606 for Party '', Service
'JDBC_Service':
Configured at 16:31:32 2006-09-08 Last message
processing started 16:47:07 2006-09-08, Error:
TransformException error in xml processor class,
rollback: Error processing request in sax parser: No
'action' attribute found in XML document (attribute
"action" missing or wrong XML structure) SXMB_MONI
says that the message has been processed
successfully.
```

Here is my source XML (XI picks this xml file thru file adapter):

```
<p2:data_filesender_MT xmlns:p2="http://filetojdbc">
<EMPID>JDK</EMPID>
<EMPNAME>JohnDoe</EMPNAME>
<EMPAGE>3</EMPAGE>
<FLAG>Yes</FLAG>
</p2:data_filesender_MT>
```

Here is my target XML (in the message mapping test window):
```
<p2:data_jdbcreceiver_MT
xmlns:p2="http://filetojdbc">
<STATEMENTNAME>
<Table1>
<action>INSERT</action>
<TABLE>Table1</TABLE>
<access>
<EMPID>JDK</EMPID>
<EMPNAME>JohnDoe</EMPNAME>
<EMPAGE>3</EMPAGE>
<FLAG>Yes</FLAG>
</access>
</Table1>
</STATEMENTNAME>
</p2:data_jdbcreceiver_MT>
```

Can you point to me what I did wrong?

A: You have created the ACTION as an element under TABLE. ACTION should be the ATTRIBUTE of the elements TABLE.

```
<p2:data_jdbcreceiver_MT
xmlns:p2="http://filetojdbc">
<STATEMENTNAME>
<Table1 action ="INSERT">
<TABLE>Table1</TABLE>
<access>
<EMPID>JDK</EMPID>
<EMPNAME>JohnDoe</EMPNAME>
<EMPAGE>3</EMPAGE>
<FLAG>Yes</FLAG>
</access>
</Table1>
</STATEMENTNAME>
</p2:data_jdbcreceiver_MT>
```

Edit the 'datatype' and make ACTION an attribute and then use the constant INSERT.

Question 74: Handling Namespaces in XSLT xpaths

I'm trying to generate the SOAP envelope using XSLT mapping. The source message to my mapping program contains two fields:

1. Username
2. PWD

But they come in with attached namespaces like ns1.

How do I specify the xpath to get the data from them?

A: You need to put the namespace declaration into the style sheet element. For example,

```
<xsl:stylesheet version="1.0"
xmlns:xsl="http://www.w3.org/1999/XSL/Transform"
xmlns:ns1="namespace1">
```

Now you can select with:

```
<xsl:value-of select="//ns1:a.username"/>
```

Question 75: Distribute SAP HR Organizational Data via SAP XI

I have to distribute the HR (SAP ERP 2005) organizational data to a SAP CRM 5.0-system via XI. Is there only one standard technology using ALE/IDocs, or are there also some other technologies available?

As I would need to change a lot in the IDoc and the concerned BAPIs, I would like to know if there are alternatives.

A: Yes, but IDocs/ALE is still the most popular interface with HR objects with ERP2005.

http://help.sap.com/saphelp_erp2005/helpdata/en/a8/ee2f37d 7e21274e10000009b38f839/frameset.htm

Still, here are some options thru XI.

1. Use of IDocs
2. Use of RFCs/BAPIs
3. Use of Proxies

It depends on the availability of the function modules in the HR side. You can think of any one of the above methods to get the data into XI. If you want to customize the BAPIs, you can plan for developing a proxy interface if feasible.

Question 76: RB_Split Option not found for Message Split

We are configuring to split a single XML with multiple records into multiple single record XML files.

During interface determination configuration, we cannot find the options for RB_Classic & RB_Split. We are on SPS17 already. Are we missing a patch of some sort? I can only see "Standard" and "Enhanced". I read somewhere that "Enhanced" is something completely different.

We already have the message mapping set up in IR. However, it looks like without this setting in ID, it is only performing the split once. So we only end up with the first record in the original message as output (5 records total).

We are simplifying our test to use 1 XML with 2 records and attempt to generate 2 single record XMLs. We are still only getting 1 output single record XML only. Our input XML looks like:

```
<ns0:MultiXML
xmlns:ns0="urn:himax:b2bi:poc:multiMapTest">
<Record>
<ID>1</ID>
<FirstName>Steve</FirstName>
<LastName>Chen</LastName>
</Record>
<Record>
<ID>2</ID>
<FirstName>Sunny</FirstName>
<LastName>Huang</LastName>
</Record>
</ns0:MultiXML>
```

and desired output is:

```
<ns0:SingleXML>
<Record>
<ID>1</ID>
<FirstName>Steve</FirstName>
<LastName>Chen</LastName>
</Record>
</ns0:MultiXML>
```

... generate as many files as the original # of records.

For mapping, I have:

```
<MultiXML> 1..1 <SingleXML> 0..unbounded (no mapping)
<Record> 1..unbounded <---> <Record> 1..1
<ID> 1..1 <---> <ID> 1..1
etc. etc.
```

Is it something to do with our occurrence settings?

A: First, a clarification. If you choose ENHANCED in INTERFACE DETERMINATION, it is used for 1: N mapping.

There is also an ENHANCED option available in Receiver Determination from Sp16 onwards, which enables you to dynamically determine receivers using a mapping.

In your case, for 1: N mapping, choose ENHANCED in INTERFACE DETERMINATION.

Also, make sure that the occurrence of the MESSAGE TYPE and MESSAGE INTERFACE in MESSAGE MAPPING and INTERFACE MAPPING has been made 1 to unbounded.

For the mapping:

<MultiXML> 1..1 <SingleXML> 0..unbounded (no mapping)

This is the problem. Map it as follows:

1. RECORD of SOURCE should be mapped to <SINGLEXML> of target.
2. RECORD of target map it to a CONSTANT.

Question 77: BPM without end

I have made a BPM. In some cases, if IDocs have not been processed in R3, this BPM will not have an end.

Is there an option that can "kill" this BPM?

A: You can use a deadline branch in which you will have to set your BPM to wait for 24 hours for an example. Inside this deadline branch, you can do something that will finish the BPM:

- Send mail for example that the BPM has finished.
- You can delete the BPM (control step - delete BPM)
- Or throw an exception (control step - throw exception)

Question 78: Monitoring SOAP Message Payload

I am doing a HTTP to SOAP scenario. I want to check if the outgoing payload (after my receiver SOAP adapter finishes processing) is correct.

--> Sent Messages / Received Messages --> Sync / Async --> Gave the valid time --> Got a list of messages.

Click on Details --> Display Message Bytes --> Display the entire SOAP message.

The Display Message Bytes displays:

```
"The message bytes for this synchronous message in
final state have been removed from the memory to save
resources".
```

I was able to see the payload for a file scenario (asynchronous). Is there any configuration that I need to do in order to see the payload for a sync call? (LOGGING_SYNC has been set to 1).

A: LOGGING_SYNC is not important with MDT.

You need to set/add in the "Messaging System" in visual admin:

messaging.syncMessageRemover.removeBody = false

Then you will see the payload.

Question 79: Java Proxies and SAP XI Document Problem

I am trying to build the application that is described in the document "Java Proxies and SAP XI Document" Part I and Part II.

In Part II I have a problem with the code of the InvokeProxy.java. In the line
```
UsersDBMTResponse_Type response = new
UsersDBMTResponse_Type();
```
"UsersDBMTResponse_Type" can not be resolved. I generated the Java Proxy from IR with both Message Interfaces. Without this java File I can't deploy the whole EJB project. I am using SPS12 and I don't know where my mistake is.

As it seems I already made a mistake in Fig. 5 of this document. I don't know how to make this IM. My IM looks different.

```
Source Interface: Users_Sync_MI
Target Interface: Users_DB_Sync_MI

Request Tab
Source Message: User_MT
Target Message: Users_DB_MT_response
Mapping Programm: Users_MM

Response Tab
Source Message: Users_DB_MT_response
Target Message: Users_DB_MT
Mapping Programm: Users_resp_MM
```

Can you help me to reach Fig. 5?

A: You need to first create three message types:

1. User_MT
2. Users_DB_MT
3. Users_DB_MT_response

Create sync o/b interface Users_Sync_MI using output message type User_MT and input message type Users_DB_MT_response.

Create sync i/b interface Users_DB_Sync_MI using input message type Users_DB_MT and output message type Users_DB_MT_response. Create message mapping as shown in Fig. 3 and Fig. 4.

Question 80: Imported RFC has problem in Converting to XML

I have a RFC with this import parameter from ABAP:

```
data: p_data type tab512 occurs 0.

Call function.......
Tables
DATA = p_data
```

This is the XML source from the mapping test in Int.Rep.

```
<?xml version="1.0" encoding="UTF-8"?>
<ns:Z_BI_SEND_DATA_512 xmlns:ns="urn:sap-
com:document:sap:rfc:functions">
<SYSID_HOME>AAA</SYSID_HOME>
<TARGETSYS>BBB</TARGETSYS>
<DATA>
<item>test1</item>
<item>test2</item>
<item>test3</item>
</DATA>
</ns:Z_BI_SEND_DATA_512>
```

This is the payload from SXMB_MONI:

```
<?xml version="1.0" encoding="UTF-8" ?>
- <rfc:Z_BI_SEND_DATA_512 xmlns:rfc="urn:sap-
com:document:sap:rfc:functions">
<SYSID_HOME>AAA</SYSID_HOME>
<TARGETSYS>BBB</TARGETSYS>
- <DATA>
- <item>
<WA>test1</WA>
</item>
- <item>
<WA>test2</WA>
</item>
- <item>
<WA>test3</WA>
```

```
</item>
</DATA>
</rfc:Z_BI_SEND_DATA_512>
```

Looks like there is a difference (imported RFC in mapping does not show the work area WA) so mapping requires:

```
<DATA>
<item>test1</item>
```

but RFC generates:

```
- <DATA>
- <item>
<WA>test1</WA>
```

Which hinders the mapping from moving the item lines into the destination file because in mapping the WA area cannot be linked as it is not recognized in mapping.

Can you suggest any possible solution to this?

A: Do not forget to activate in SAP BASIS SWCV the element for the substructure "WA" which is the table reference for the data element "item" in your RFC. Then, import your RFC again.

Question 81: Problem in Integration Directory after Transport

We did a SLD transport (only LD objects), with DEV and PRD groups. It had some error messages because the SWCVs from the Dev XI were not created into PRD XI. But despite the errors, the products and SWCV's were created.

After that, we've done IR and ID objects transports, through File System. Apparently, the IR part was OK.

In the ID, it correctly changed the Business Systems from Dev Configuration to their respective transport targets. However, if we try to open any Adapter, it gives an error message:

"Attempt to access the 1 requested objects on 1 failed. Detailed information: com.sap.aii.ib.core.roa.RoaObjectAccessException: Unable to read object Adapter Metadata SOAP | http://sap.com/xi/XI/System (b38bcd00-e471-11d7-afac-de420a1145a5) of type AdapterMetaData from application REPOSITORY on system REPOSITORY. Detailed information: Software component version with GUID b38bcd00-e471-11d7-afac-de420a1145a5 does not exist"

We tried to create a new Adapter, but when we get to select adapter type (SOAP, File, RFC, etc.) it says:

"Search Result for All Component Versions
No objects found!"

So, we can't select any adapter type.

Can you help us correct this problem?

A: You need to import the SAP BASIS 6.4 or 7.0 Software Component Version into Integration Repository.

For this ".tpz" file you can get from:

Copy XI3_0_SAP_BASIS_6.40_09_00.tpz from <Components DVD>/XI /XI_CONTENT to directory /usr/sap/<SAPSID>/SYS/global/xi/repository_server/import/

Question 82: SWCV

In a SAP XI .NET scenario, what are the SWCV that has to be imported from SLD?

A: There are no standard software components to be imported from SLD. You need to define what components you will need for your scenario.

Let us say you created a software component SAP_2_NET in SLD; you then will need to import this SWC into repository for implementation in your scenario.

Question 83: Creating a "less than" Condition in the Condition Editor

I'm designing a BPM with a loop that needs to run while a counter is less than a determined value.

I have defined the counter as a simple type container and used a container operator to increment this counter. But in the condition editor for the loop, I did not find a simple way to create this "less than" condition, other than creating a huge OR statement with all the possible values that the counter can assume (1, 2, up to max_value), which I would really rather not to use.

I read about using a XPath expression to create this less than condition, but I need to use it in a simple variable, not a message.

I've also searched through SDN about this, but I didn't manage to find anything on the topic (except for the XPath thing).

Is there any way of doing this?

A: Don't use the "NOT EQUAL TO" in your condition editor.

Initialize the variable to the maximum value and then decrement it. Once it reaches the minimum value for which "NOT EQUAL TO" is defined, it will stop processing and get out of the SWITCH and so on.

The condition editor is used in your BPM only for LOOP (SWITCH STEP).

For additional reference visit:

http://help.sap.com/saphelp_nw04/helpdata/en/67/49767669 963545a071a190b77a9a23/content.htm

http://help.sap.com/saphelp_nw04/helpdata/en/ab/13bf7191e7 3a4fb3560e767a2525fd/content.htm

Question 84: Call the Method on the Object Externally

We have several external non-SAP applications that work online with our SAP system by mean of RFC calls and BAPI calls (using JCO).

BAPI is technically a RFC function, so it makes no difference to the caller that it calls an RFC function or a BAPI. But, a BAPI is also a method on a Business Object.

Is it possible to call the method on the object externally (using JCO or other connector)?

Instead of exposing the implementation of the BAPI (thus the RFC function), I would like to instantiate the Business Object and call its method. Is it possible from outside SAP?

A: No. It is not possible to expose the business object method or its implementation from outside SAP.

A business object method can be implemented in several ways: Function module, API function, Transaction, Dialog module, Report or other.

Thus using JCo or another RFC library should enable you to access the method regarding its implementation.

For implementations of type Report or Transaction this seems very unlikely since a front-end is required.

Question 85: Alert Inbox - One Message

I configured the alert inbox to work. When an error is received, I see it in the alert inbox. However, if another error is received, I don't get any alerts anymore for the same interface.

How do I configure the alert inbox to give an alert for every error?

A: In your ALERT RULE, you must have selected the option,

```
"SUPRESS MULTIPLE ALERTS OF THIS RULE"
```

You need to unselect this option, and you will get the alert every time the error occurs for that interface.

Question 86: Calling a RFC from a BPM Process

I have a question about calling a RFC from a BPM process using a synchronous call. When I go to review the graphical workflow log, I can see that the synchronous send task is completed; but when I look at the messages processed by the integration server in SXMB_MONI, I cannot see the successful message sent by my abstract BPM interface. I think that I have all of the receiver determination and interface mappings between the abstract BPM send interface and the inbound RFC interface. The interesting part is that the only time when I can see the message in SXMB_MONI is when I break the interface mapping between the abstract and inbound interfaces.

Do you have any ideas what causes this?

A: You can always see all of the steps of the BMP by clicking PE (in the message monitoring) then "list with technical details" (not the graphical workflow) and then "show item container" on the send step, or mapping, or anything else (the one where you can see all of the XML messages involved).

You can also use TCODE: SXMS_SAMON. It shows the number of active sync calls waiting for a response.

If you have not set logging for synchronous messages, they will not show up in the SXMB_MONI unless they are in error.

To set it up, go to transaction sxmb_adm Configuration, then to "Integration Engine Configuration" then "Change Specific Configuration Data".

```
Category  : Runtime
Parameter : LOGGING_SYNC
value : 1 (activated)
```

Question 87: Generic Integration

If you a have a non-SAP system (like Oracle forms based application using oracle DB) that is not SOAP/HTTP/JMS capable how can I have that system push a message out to SAP through XI?

A: Your best option will be to use XI JDBC adapter read a database on that system and send the message to XI.

File and JDBC adapter are the most commonly used. There is also JMS, which is often used with older systems, e.g. mainframe applications, putting messages into a queue which XI will read.

For some systems which are quite common (like Oracle Financials, JDEdwards etc.) 3rd party adapters are available from "Iway" and "Seeburger" mainly. These adapters are sold by SAP and support will also be provided through SAP OSS. Check out the "Connectivity Section" at:

http://service.sap.com/xi

Following that, you can always implement a specific adapter if this system has some possibility to extract data, e.g. your own API. IMO is the last resort if you can't use any of the standard adapters, as it requires more effort.

Question 88: Faulty message handling in BPM

I created a business process with a synchronous sending step. I defined all interfaces and implemented an 'own fault message' type within the synchronous abstract interface. If the used RFC got the correct data, the sync sending step works properly and the business process works fine also. If I provide wrong data to the RFC to force it to throw an exception, the 'Business' process receives the fault message.

I just want to send the received fault message asynchronously to a file adapter within the defined exception branch. I was not able to implement a new variable in the container for the fault message type.

How can I still send the message?

A: No, you cannot send the message. It is definitely not possible to further process the content of the exception message within the exception branch. The exception message received by the BPM only triggers the exception branch. The message itself cannot be defined as an abstract interface.

Question 89: SAP R3 to Legacy System Including Master Data Using XI

I am doing integration from SAP R3 to Legacy system including master data (customer, Material, BOM etc).

Is there any way through an ALE setup that I can send master data (create/change) to Legacy system real time?

A: Yes. This type of scenarios is an R/3->XI->Legacy Systems. In this case R/3 can give the data in different formats either Idoc/RFC/ABAP Proxy. There are some standard IDocs available for this in R/3 (BOM,Material). You can make use of this to configure your IDOC->XI->Legacy System (File) scenario.

When you are talking about Master Data, then you have MDM in your Design. In this case, you can use XI for distributing data into legacy systems.

Whenever you change, for example PO, data has to automatically update and there are some standard Idocs from SAP (ORDERS, CHNG). Whenever it triggers that Idoc, you need to make sure that it should reach XI. For this, you need to fill control record information like logical system, port etc. This scenario is of adHoc type. You can even schedule the Idoc processing once in a day, etc.

Question 90: Webservice

I am working on a Webservice scenario. I created a RFC function module and converted the same to Webservice. But while creating communication channels, I need to pass the target URL.

I passed the URL location, but I got the following error message:

```
* * * * * * * * * * * * * * * *
<?xml version="1.0" encoding="UTF-8" standalone="yes"
?>
- <!-- Call Adapter
-->
- <SAP:Error
xmlns:SAP="http://sap.com/xi/XI/Message/30"
xmlns:SOAP="http://schemas.xmlsoap.org/soap/envelope/
" SOAP:mustUnderstand="1">
<SAP:Category>XIAdapter</SAP:Category>
<SAP:Code
area="PARSING">ADAPTER.SOAP_EXCEPTION</SAP:Code>
<SAP:P1 />
<SAP:P2 />
<SAP:P3 />
<SAP:P4 />
<SAP:AdditionalText>soap fault: SOAP processing
failure, error id = 1001</SAP:AdditionalText>
<SAP:ApplicationFaultMessage namespace="" />
<SAP:Stack />
<SAP:Retry>M</SAP:Retry>
</SAP:Error>
* * * * * * * * * * * * * * * *
```

Can you help me solve this problem?

A: The information below will surely help you find an answer.

If you are on WAS 6.20 and up, you can expose an RFC as a webservice directly from WAS.

If you're on Basis layer 4.6D, you will need to use XI (or some other integration tool) to expose the RFC as a webservice.

To do this in XI you'll need to do the following:

Integration Repository

1. Import the RFC
2. Define a message and datatype for the SOAP interface
3. Create inbound and outbound interfaces
4. Create maps between the RFC and SOAP messages
5. Create an interface map.

Integration Directory

1. Create an RFC Receiver Channel
2. Create a SOAP Sender Channel
3. Generate the WSDL (Tools->Define Web Service).

You can then hand off the WSDL and a login username and password to your developer and they will have everything they need to make the WS call.

Here are answers to a few questions that might arise.

1. Do I need to actually create a WS that calls the RFC? Isn't the virtual interface exposed by the XI sufficient?

   Yes, you need to create a WS in XI that calls the RFC.

2. If I really have to create the WS and deploy it in order to expose it with the XI, then what is my benefit of exposing it with the XI? Why not just expose it as a normal WS?

   You don't have WAS 6.20 or up. Even if you did, you may still want to expose it using XI in order to have all of your integration go through the same application.

3. If I expose my web service through the XI, how does the client application executes one of its methods? To which url does it have to access (the XI or the actual WS)?

    You expose a SOAP interface in XI by generating a WSDL file. This file contains all of the information a developer will need to call the webservice including the URL.

    You actually specify the URL when you generate the WSDL. Be sure to read the documentation to get the correct format because the URL that the wizard suggests isn't correct.

Question 91: Polling Interval

How do you set a polling interval, in case of IDoc to file scenario? How about in other scenarios?

A: There is actually no need to set a polling interval for an IDoc to file scenario. Interval/s will be set when you need to pick the file and sent into XI, for example, when your scenario is like File to XI to IDoc/RFC etc.

In your IDoc to File scenario, your IDoc will be triggered from your external system, and there is no sender IDoc adapter, so there is obviously no polling interval for the same.

In the case of your file, as the file adapter is a receiver file adapter, it will generate your file whenever the IDoc is triggered from your external system and so no polling interval is also required for the receiver file adapter.

In the case of File to XI to IDoc, the polling interval will have to be specified in your File Adapter. Now, the interval to be mentioned depends on how often you want the file adapter to scan and search for files.

If you say, 10 seconds, then the adapter will poll every 10 seconds for the file. So, the poll interval you give will be purely on how often the file is to be picked by XI and passed as an IDoc to the external system.

In the case of a File to IDoc scenario, the XI Sender File Adapter picks up the file to send to the target/receiving system. The Sender File Adapter can be configured to poll at regular intervals. The polling interval can be set as per the schedule of the extract program. In case the extract is on-demand, then you can set the polling interval to 60 secs or 600 secs. The point is that the interface can be triggered by the File Adapter polling mechanism.

There are a few parameters that you define while configuring the Sender File/FTP Adapter, so I thought I will just tell you what exactly a few of them relating to polling time mean:

1. Poll Interval (secs) - Number of seconds that the adapter must wait if no files are found for processing.

2. Poll Interval (msecs) - Additional waiting time in milliseconds.

    a. If Poll Interval (secs) is set to null, processing times will be short and close to real time.
    b. If Poll Interval (secs) and Poll Interval (msecs) are set to null, the adapter is only called once.

3. Retry Interval (secs) - Specify the number of seconds that the adapter is to wait before a file processed with errors is processed again.

    a. If the value is set to null, then the adapter is canceled if an error occurs, even if a value greater than null is specified for Poll Interval (secs).

While configuring a sender file adapter, a common major mistake is keeping file adapter communication channel polling interval less and in test mode. It is not an error, keeping it in test mode with less polling interval but, often it is forgotten, keeping the adapter channel active and it loads the server memory unnecessarily.

Question 92: JDBC Java SQL Exception Error

I received t the following SQL error for the JDBC adapter.

```
TransformException error in xml processor class:
Error processing request in sax parser: Error when
executing statement for table/stored proc. 'CUSTOMER'
(structure 'statementname'): java.sql.SQLException:
[SQL7008] TEST1 in QGPL not valid for operation.
```

The following is the XML message payload:

```
<?xml version="1.0" encoding="utf-8" ?>
- <ns1:TESTCUSTOMER
xmlns:ns1="http://test.com/xi/JDBC">
- <statementname>
- <CUSTOMER action="insert">
- <access>
<TEST1>100</TEST1>
</access>
</CUSTOMER>
</statementname>
</ns1:TESTCUSTOMER>
```

CUSTOMER is the name of the TABLE. TEST1 is a column existing in the table.

I wrote a JAVA programmed to insert the data into the table using the same JDBC driver and it worked fine.

Can you help me make this work?

A: Use this setting to see the SQL coming out of your adapter, refer to note: 801367.

JDBC Receiver Adapter Parameters:

1. Parameter name: "logSQLStatement"
Parameter type: boolean

Parameter value: true for any string value, false only for empty string

Parameter value default: false (empty String)

Available with: SP9

Category: 2

Description:

When implementing a scenario with the JDBC receiver adapter, it may be helpful to see which SQL statement is generated by the JDBC adapter from the XI message content for error analysis. Before SP9, this can only be found in the trace of the JDBC adapter if trace level DEBUG is activated. With SP9, the generated SQL statement will be shown in the details page (audit protocol) of the message monitor for each message directly.

This should be used only during the test phase and not in productive scenarios.

The error was due to the commit in the database. You did not use any parameters in the Advance Mode.

Question 93: Problem with BPM Starting

I defined a BPM Object. Message has been received correctly, but no instances of the BPM have been started. I simulated the same BPM with another old XI System and it works.

The error is an "Outbound Error" in the monitor (red flag).

What can be the cause of this and how do I solve it?

A: You will need to check up SXI_CACHE to see if your BPM is enabled. See what the return code is; it should be "0". If the value is not "0", try activating BPM from there.

Question 94: Sales Document Type not defined

I am working on an interface, which is designed as follows.

Purchase Order->File Adapter->XI (BPM) ->RFC Adapter->Sales Order in R/3

When I tried to create a sales document in R/3, I got a message back from R/3 saying "Sales Document is not defined", but when checked in R/3, that sales document type exist. I don't see any mapping exception in monitoring.

I used a standard BAPI called BAPI_SALESORDER_PROXY_CREATE for sales order creation. In my input xml file, I have a value for a field called 'DocTypeCode' as 'Z4OR'. I ran the test even without this filed value and it gave me the same message.

Initially it was a value-mapping problem.

Is it possible to debug a BAPI/RFC from XI?

If it is possible, please advise me of the procedure. My XI is working fine but I am getting a message back from R/3 as follows:

```
<?xml version="1.0" encoding="UTF-8" ?>
- <rfc:BAPI_SALESORDER_PROXY_CREATE.Response
xmlns:rfc="urn:sap-com:document:sap:rfc:functions">
<E_SALESDOCUMENT_EX />
<E_STATUS>E</E_STATUS>
- <RETURN>
- <item>
<TYPE>S</TYPE>
<ID>V4</ID>
<NUMBER>233</NUMBER>
<MESSAGE>SALES_HEADER_IN has been processed
successfully</MESSAGE>
<LOG_NO />
<LOG_MSG_NO>000000</LOG_MSG_NO>
<MESSAGE_V1>VBAKKOM</MESSAGE_V1>
<MESSAGE_V2 />
<MESSAGE_V3 />
<MESSAGE_V4 />
<PARAMETER>SALES_HEADER_IN</PARAMETER>
<ROW>0</ROW>
<FIELD />
<SYSTEM>UD1CLNT010</SYSTEM>
</item>
- <item>
<TYPE>E</TYPE>
<ID>V1</ID>
<NUMBER>384</NUMBER>
<MESSAGE>Sales unit ****** is not defined for item
000000</MESSAGE>
<LOG_NO />
<LOG_MSG_NO>000000</LOG_MSG_NO>
<MESSAGE_V1>******</MESSAGE_V1>
<MESSAGE_V2>000000</MESSAGE_V2>
<MESSAGE_V3 />
<MESSAGE_V4 />
<PARAMETER>SALES_ITEM_IN</PARAMETER>
<ROW>1</ROW>
<FIELD />
<SYSTEM>UD1CLNT010</SYSTEM>
</item>
- <item>
<TYPE>E</TYPE>
<ID>V4</ID>
<NUMBER>248</NUMBER>
```

```
<MESSAGE>Error in SALES_ITEM_IN 000001</MESSAGE>
<LOG_NO />
<LOG_MSG_NO>000000</LOG_MSG_NO>
<MESSAGE_V1>VBAPKOM</MESSAGE_V1>
<MESSAGE_V2>000001</MESSAGE_V2>
<MESSAGE_V3 />
<MESSAGE_V4 />
<PARAMETER>SALES_ITEM_IN</PARAMETER>
<ROW>1</ROW>
<FIELD />
<SYSTEM>UD1CLNT010</SYSTEM>
</item>
- <item>
<TYPE>E</TYPE>
<ID>V4</ID>
<NUMBER>219</NUMBER>
<MESSAGE>Sales document was not changed</MESSAGE>
<LOG_NO />
<LOG_MSG_NO>000000</LOG_MSG_NO>
<MESSAGE_V1 />
<MESSAGE_V2>000001</MESSAGE_V2>
<MESSAGE_V3 />
<MESSAGE_V4 />
<PARAMETER />
<ROW>0</ROW>
<FIELD />
<SYSTEM>UD1CLNT010</SYSTEM>
</item>
- <item>
<TYPE>E</TYPE>
<ID>C_</ID>
<NUMBER>005</NUMBER>
<MESSAGE>The object references could not be written
to the CRMKEY</MESSAGE>
<LOG_NO />
<LOG_MSG_NO>000000</LOG_MSG_NO>
<MESSAGE_V1 />
<MESSAGE_V2 />
<MESSAGE_V3 />
<MESSAGE_V4 />
<PARAMETER />
<ROW>0</ROW>
<FIELD />
<SYSTEM>UD1CLNT010</SYSTEM>
</item>
</RETURN>
<TI_EXTENSIONIN />
<TI_ORDER_CCARD />
<TI_ORDER_CFGS_BLOB />
```

```
<TI_ORDER_CFGS_INST />
<TI_ORDER_CFGS_PART_OF />
<TI_ORDER_CFGS_REF />
<TI_ORDER_CFGS_REFINST />
<TI_ORDER_CFGS_VALUE />
<TI_ORDER_CFGS_VK />
- <TI_ORDER_CONDITIONS_IN>
- <item>
<ITM_NUMBER>000001</ITM_NUMBER>
<COND_ST_NO>000</COND_ST_NO>
<COND_COUNT>00</COND_COUNT>
<COND_TYPE>EDI1</COND_TYPE>
<COND_VALUE>57.600000000</COND_VALUE>
<CURRENCY>AUD</CURRENCY>
<COND_UNIT />
<COND_P_UNT>1</COND_P_UNT>
<CURR_ISO />
<CD_UNT_ISO />
<REFOBJTYPE />
<REFOBJKEY />
<REFLOGSYS />
<APPLICATIO />
```

A: You can't debug an R/3 RFC from XI. This looks like a data problem based on message: <MESSAGE>Sales unit ****** is not defined for item 000000</MESSAGE>

The UOM you are sending in for the material is not valid.

You will need to remove the UOM from the input xml instance and pass the data through.

Question 95: Global Data Types

We have complex types that we would like to use across software components. I want to create a data type that references a data type outside the current SWC.

Is this possible?

A: Yes, it is possible. I just tested one a few weeks ago. Let me explain with an example:

SWC:A (contains the data type which you want to reference, say, include_DT)
SWC:B (contains the data type where you want to reference a DT which is in SWC:A. Lets call it Main_DT).

You need to create the dependency between SWC:A and SWC:B in the SLD.

While creating the Main_DT, you will have to use "Search Help" to reference the include_DT in any of the sub-elements that you have. But you cannot reference the include_DT at the root element level in Main_DT.

Question 96: IDoc to R/3

I need to check the IDoc sent from XI to R/3. I need to see the results and verify if there are any errors.

How can I do this?

A: You need to go to transaction we02/we05. On the left of the screen, double click on the IDoc type that you sent. A list of transactions will be displayed; check the IDoc corresponding to your scenario, and check if it is green.

Sm58 is the tRFC queue and check if there are some entries. Only errors are recorded there. If there is no entry for your IDoc here, then, your scenario is successful.

You may want to take a look at this link. It will help you understand where you can look if an error occurred.

Question 97: "Scheduled for outbound processing" Message

My scenario is:

```
R/3 (IDoc Customer) -> XI -> PC (file)
```

I use a BPM with option "multi to single".

In the Message Monitoring, I have two steps:

1.   Idoc DEBMAS06 --> BPM: status = "Processed successfully".
2.   BPM --> my PC: status = "Scheduled for Outbound processing" and in column "outbound" I have not "IENGINE". There is no other error message and obviously no data are sent to my PC.

I have checked transaction SMQ2. I can see that queue status = "SYSFAIL" and I have two types of messages:

```
- XI Error CLIENT_RECEIVE_FAILED.INTERNAL: Queue stop
- XI restart in qRFC not allowed.
```

Can you help me sort this out?

A: Yes. First, reset the status to "Ready".

Then if you get SYSFAIL again, delete that particular LUW. If there are other messages waiting in the queue, just click on the unlock queue button and the remaining messages will flow thru.

Question 98: Conversion Agent - Integration with XI / SP15

I am trying to evaluate the features of the Conversion Agent and its usage within XI / SP15 (Windows based).

I did the first CA HL7 tutorial and deployed the correct transformation script as Conversion Agent "Service" named "HL7_Parsing_Test". When I tried to run the Service via the "CM_Console", everything was passed successfully.

However, when I tried to include the service in our File Sender Adapter which parses the same HL7 source file, I got a "NullPointerException" (and the File Sender Adapter went to red light).

I added the Conversion Agent "CMTransformBean" to our communication channel and set the parameter "TransformationName" to the value "HL7_Parsing_Test" without success.

The exact configuration is as follows:

1.   Added Modulname: "localejbs/sap.com/com.sap.nw.cm.xi/CMTransformBean" (JNDI-Name of CMTransformBean). Type of Bean = "Local Enterprise Bean"
2.   Parametername: "TransformationName"
3.   Parameter value: "HL7_Parsing_Test"

How do you successfully include the CMtransformBean into an XI communication channel?

A: You need to check whether you added the CMtransformBean before the CallSapAdapter Bean in the module chain, and not after it. Placing the CMtransformBean after the CallSapAdapter Bean causes the above error that you encountered.

Question 99: Soap Error: Content-Type of the Request should be Text/XML

I am working on a HTTP-SOAP scenario and I have checked the "Do not use SOAP Envelope" check box, in the receiver soap adapter. I created the message payload with the SOAP envelope in the interface mapping.

When I sent a request to the webservice, I got the following error:

```
<faultcode>soapenv:Client</faultcode>
<faultstring>content-type of the request should be
text/xml</faultstring>
```

When I checked the message payload in MDT, I found that an extra soap envelope is added by the adapter in spite of the setting made in the receiver soap adapter. This extra soap envelope has content-type as application/xml and hence the error.

Here is the payload:

```
--SAP_3c63dd11-369b-11db-902c-0002559ad50b_END
Content-ID: <soap-
3c63dd10369b11dba74e0002559ad50b@sap.com>
Content-Disposition: attachment;filename="soap-
3c63dd10369b11dba74e0002559ad50b@sap.com.xml"
Content-Type: text/xml; charset=utf-8
Content-Description: SOAP


--------Begin of extra soap envelope--------

<SOAP:Envelope
xmlns:SOAP='http://schemas.xmlsoap.org/soap/envelope/
'>
<SOAP:Header
xmlns:xlink='http://www.w3.org/1999/xlink'
xmlns:SAP='http://sap.com/xi/XI/Message/30'
xmlns:wsse='http://www.docs.oasis-
open.org/wss/2004/01/oasis-200401-wss-wssecurity-
secext-1.0.xsd'>
<SAP:Main versionMajor='3' versionMinor='0'
SOAP:mustUnderstand='1'
xmlns:wsu='http://www.docs.oasis-
```

```
open.org/wss/2004/01/oasis-200401-wss-wssecurity-
utility-1.0.xsd' wsu:Id='wsuid-main-
92ABE13F5C59AB7FE10000000A1551F7'>
<SAP:MessageClass>ApplicationMessage</SAP:MessageClas
s>
<SAP:ProcessingMode>synchronous</SAP:ProcessingMode>
<SAP:MessageId>44f2ef85-b9e1-0045-0000-
0000911aa04f</SAP:MessageId>
<SAP:TimeSent>2006-08-28T13:43:28Z</SAP:TimeSent>
<SAP:Sender><SAP:Party agency=''
scheme=''></SAP:Party>
<SAP:Service>HTTPSENDER</SAP:Service>
</SAP:Sender>
<SAP:Receiver><SAP:Party agency='' scheme=''>
</SAP:Party><SAP:Service>SOAPRECEIVER</SAP:Service></
SAP:Receiver><SAP:Interface
namespace='urn:horizon:sforce'>MI_SFORCE</SAP:Interfa
ce></SAP:Main><SAP:ReliableMessaging
SOAP:mustUnderstand='1'><SAP:QualityOfService>BestEff
ort</SAP:QualityOfService></SAP:ReliableMessaging><SA
P:Diagnostic
SOAP:mustUnderstand='1'><SAP:TraceLevel>Fatal</SAP:Tr
aceLevel><SAP:Logging>Off</SAP:Logging></SAP:Diagnost
ic><SAP:HopList SOAP:mustUnderstand='1'><SAP:Hop
timeStamp='2006-08-28T13:43:28Z'
wasRead='false'><SAP:Engine
type='IS'></SAP:Engine><SAP:Adapter
namespace='http://sap.com/xi/XI/System'>HTTP</SAP:Ada
pter><SAP:MessageId>44f2ef85-b9e1-0045-0000-
0000911aa04f</SAP:MessageId><SAP:Info>host:ztm0042.se
rvices.shell.net:8005::remote-
addr:145.30.233.51</SAP:Info></SAP:Hop><SAP:Hop
timeStamp='2006-08-28T13:43:28Z'
wasRead='false'><SAP:Engine
type='IS'>is.05.ztm0042</SAP:Engine><SAP:Adapter
namespace='http://sap.com/xi/XI/System'>XI</SAP:Adapt
er><SAP:MessageId>44f2ef85-b9e1-0045-0000-
0000911aa04f</SAP:MessageId><SAP:Info>3.0</SAP:Info><
/SAP:Hop><SAP:Hop timeStamp='2006-08-28T13:43:30Z'
wasRead='false'><SAP:Engine
type='AF'>af.dx5.ztm0042</SAP:Engine><SAP:Adapter
namespace='http://sap.com/xi/XI/System'>XIRA</SAP:Ada
pter><SAP:MessageId>44f2ef85-b9e1-0045-0000-
0000911aa04f</SAP:MessageId></SAP:Hop></SAP:HopList><
/SOAP:Header><SOAP:Body><sap:Manifest
xmlns:sap='http://sap.com/xi/XI/Message/30'
xmlns:xlink='http://www.w3.org/1999/xlink'
xmlns:wsu='http://www.docs.oasis-
open.org/wss/2004/01/oasis-200401 wss-wssecurity-
```

```
utility-1.0.xsd' wsu:Id='wsuid-manifest-
5CABE13F5C59AB7FE10000000A1551F7'><sap:Payload
xlink:type='simple' xlink:href='cid:payload-
44F2EF86B9E10045000000000911AA04F@sap.com'><sap:Name>M
ainDocument</sap:Name><sap:Description></sap:Descript
ion><sap:Type>Application</sap:Type></sap:Payload></s
ap:Manifest></SOAP:Body></SOAP:Envelope>
--SAP_3c63dd11-369b-11db-902c-0002559ad50b_END
content-id: payload-
44F2EF86B9E10045000000000911AA04F@sap.com
content-type: application/xml;charset=UTF-8

------End of extra soap envelope-----------
```

------Below is the expected payload, generated using xsl--

```
<?xml version="1.0" encoding="utf-8"?>
<soap:Envelope
xmlns:soap="http://schemas.xmlsoap.org/soap/envelope/
" xmlns:xsi="http://www.w3.org/2001/XMLSchema-
instance"
xmlns:xsd="http://www.w3.org/2001/XMLSchema">
<soap:Body>
<ns1:login
xmlns:ns1="urn:enterprise.soap.sforce.com">
<ns1:username>apiabc</ns1:username>
<ns1:password>123</ns1:password>
</ns1:login>
</soap:Body>
</soap:Envelope>

--SAP_3c63dd11-369b-11db-902c-0002559ad50b_END-
```

Can you give any help on this?

A: Yes. You need to add "&nosoap=true" in the receiver soap
adapter target URL.

Question 100: Problem Exporting XML via RFC

I used RFC to send XML data from CRM to XI. My function module (/MARS/CPE_IMPORT_CRM_CATALOG) contains only one parameter (IV_CATALOG) declared as a string so all XML data is placed in this string.

I tried sending the following string from CRM:

<TEST>GREG</TEST>

The payload on XI looks like this:

```
<xml version="1.0" encoding="UTF-8"?>
<rfc:_-MARS_-CPE_IMPORT_CRM_CATALOG
xmlns:rfc="urn:sap-com:document:sap:rfc:functions">
<IV_CATALOG>&#60;TEST&#62;GREG&#60;/TEST&#62;</IV_CAT
ALOG></rfc:_-MARS_-CPE_IMPORT_CRM_CATALOG>
```

We can see < is converted into < and > into >

Where and how do I specify that the content of the parameter must not be interpreted?

A: The RFC adapter serializes the content of the parameters (for instance the characters < and >) in order to avoid conflicts with real XML tags, as you can easily create non-valid XML.

Add the following mapping between the adapter and your real mapping. This mapping simply converts the < resp. > into < resp. >. It is then possible to send XML into the RFC parameters. If the XML sent in the parameter is not well formed, XI will reject the message.

```java
package com.sap.mymappings;

import java.io.BufferedReader;
import java.io.IOException;
import java.io.InputStream;
import java.io.InputStreamReader;
import java.io.OutputStream;
import java.util.Map;

import com.sap.aii.mapping.api.StreamTransformation;

public class DecodeXml implements
StreamTransformation {
private Map map;
private OutputStream out;

/**
*
*/
public DecodeXml() {
super();
// Auto-generated constructor stub
}

/**
* method setParamters is required, but we do not
anything with it
*/
public void setParameter(Map param) {
map = param;
}

/**
* method execute is called by the XI mapping program
*/
public void execute(InputStream in, OutputStream out)
throws
com.sap.aii.mapping.api.StreamTransformationException
{
InputStreamReader inReader = new
InputStreamReader(in);
```

```
// 2. Helper classes to read in data
BufferedReader bufReader = new
BufferedReader(inReader);
String s;
String helpString = new String();
String resString = new String();

int i = 0;
try {
while ((s = bufReader.readLine()) != null) {
helpString = s.replaceAll("&#60;", "<");
helpString = helpString.replaceAll("&#62;", ">");
resString = resString + helpString;
i++;
}
} catch (IOException e) {
// TODO Auto-generated catch block
e.printStackTrace();
}
try {
bufReader.close();
} catch (IOException e1) {
// TODO Auto-generated catch block
e1.printStackTrace();
}

// 4. Write data to OutputStream
byte[] resByte = resString.getBytes();
try {
out.write(resByte, 0, resByte.length);
} catch (IOException e2) {
// TODO Auto-generated catch block
e2.printStackTrace();
}

}
```

Acronyms:

ABAP - Advanced Business Application Programming
BAPI - Business Application Programming Interface
BPM - Business Process Management
CC - Communication Channel
CMS - Change Management Service
LUW - Logical Units of Work
NWDS - NetWeaver Developer Studio
OSS - Online Service System
RFC - Remote Function Call
RWB – Runtime Workbench
SLD - System Landscape Directory
SOAP - Simple Object Access Protocol (XML protocol)
SSL – Secured Socket Layer
SWCV - Software Component Versions
UME - User Management Engine
UOM - Unit Of Measure
VPN - Virtual Private Network
WSDL - Web Services Description Language (XML format)
XML - Extensible Markup Language
XSLT - Extensible Stylesheet Language Transformations

INDEX

Printed in the United States
112730LV00001B/82/P